ELINES
OF
HISTORY
VOLUME 2

THE CLASSICAL AGE

500 B.C.–500 A.D.

GROLIER

an imprint of

SCHOLASTIC

www.scholastic.com/librarypublishing

Published by Grolier,
an imprint of Scholastic Library Publishing,
Sherman Turnpike
Danbury, Connecticut 06816

© 2005 The Brown Reference Group plc

Set ISBN 0-7172-6002-X
Volume 2 ISBN 0-7172-6004-6

Library of Congress Cataloging-in-Publication Data

Timelines of history.
        p. cm.
    Includes index.
    Contents: v. 1. The early empires, prehistory—500 B.C. —
v. 2. The classical age, 500 B.C.—500 A.D. — v. 3. Raiders and
conquerors, 500—1000 — v. 4. The feudal era, 1000—1250 —
v. 5. The end of the Middle Ages, 1250—1500 — v. 6. A wider
world, 1500—1600 — v. 7. Royalty and revolt, 1600—1700 —
v. 8. The Age of Reason, 1700—1800 — v. 9. Industry and
empire, 1800—1900 — v. 10. The modern world, 1900—2000.
    ISBN 0-7172-6002-X (set : alk. paper) — ISBN 0-7172-
6003-8 (v. 1 : alk. paper) — ISBN 0-7172-6004-6 (v. 2 : alk.
paper) — ISBN 0-7172-6005-4 (v. 3 : alk. paper) — ISBN 0-
7172-6006-2 (v. 4 : alk. paper) — ISBN 0-7172-6007-0 (v. 5 :
alk. paper) — ISBN 0-7172-6008-9 (v. 6 : alk. paper) — ISBN
0-7172-6009-7 (v. 7 : alk. paper) — ISBN 0-7172-6010-0 (v. 8
: alk.paper) — ISBN 0-7172-6011-9 (v. 9 : alk. paper) —
ISBN 0-7172-6012-7 (v. 10 : alk. paper)
    1. Chronology, Historical

For information address the publisher:
Grolier, Sherman Turnpike,
Danbury, Connecticut 06816

Printed and bound in Thailand

FOR THE BROWN REFERENCE GROUP PLC

Consultant: Professor Jeremy Black, University of Exeter

Project Editor: Tony Allan
Designers: Frankie Wood
Picture Researcher: Sharon Southren
Cartographic Editor: Tim Williams
Design Manager: Lynne Ross
Production: Alastair Gourlay, Maggie Copeland
Senior Managing Editor: Tim Cooke
Editorial Director: Lindsey Lowe
Writers: Windsor Chorlton, Penny Isaacs, Susan Kennedy,
Michael Kerrigan

PICTURE CREDITS
(t = top, b = bottom, c = center, l = left, r = right)

Cover
Corbis: Christie's Images b.

AKG-images: 13cr, 45b; ©**Philip Baird/ www.
anthroarcheart.org:** 43b; **Corbis:** 18t, Archivo Iconografico, S.A.
31c, Bettmann 11cl, 19, 22t, Eye Ubiquitous/Hugh Rooney 38,
Jack Field 14bl, Chris Hellier 43t, Dewitt Jones 26t, Wolfgang
Kaehler 7t, Liu Ligun 22b, Royal Ontario Museum 34b,
Sakamoto Photo Research Laboratory 20; **Robert Harding
Picture Library:** ImageState 16c, J.H.C. Wilson 37; **Zev
Radovan:** 33; **TopFoto.co.uk:** HIP 18b.

The Brown Reference Group has made every effort to trace
copyright holders of the pictures used in this book. Anyone
having claims to ownership not identified above is invited to
contact The Brown Reference Group.

CONTENTS

How to Use This Book   4

TIMELINE: 500–400 B.C.   6

THE GREEK CITY-STATES   8

TIMELINE: 400–300 B.C.   10

ALEXANDER THE GREAT   12

TIMELINE: 300–200 B.C.   14

CHINA'S FIRST EMPEROR   16

TIMELINE: 200–100 B.C.   18

THE GROWTH OF BUDDHISM   20

TIMELINE: 100 B.C.–0   22

THE RISE OF ROME   24

TIMELINE: 0–100 A.D.   26

THE ROMAN EMPIRE   28

TIMELINE: 100–200 A.D.   30

THE JEWISH DIASPORA   32

TIMELINE: 200–300 A.D.   34

THE INDIAN EMPIRES   36

TIMELINE: 300–400 A.D.   38

THE SPREAD OF CHRISTIANITY   40

TIMELINE: 400–500 A.D.   42

THE FALL OF THE ROMAN EMPIRE   44

Facts at a Glance   46

Further Reading   54

Set Index   54

HOW TO USE THIS BOOK

INTRODUCTION

The timelines of history in this volume begin with the birth of democracy in the city-states of Greece around 500 B.C. The civilization of ancient Greece was one of the most remarkable in history; the legacy of its achievements in politics, art, literature, and philosophy is still felt today. By the 2nd century B.C. Greece had been surpassed by the military might of the Romans. They went on to found one of the greatest empires the world had yet seen, stretching right around the shores of the Mediterranean and across western Europe; but by 500 A.D. the empire had collapsed, its western territories overrun by barbarian invaders.

The thousand years encompassed by these two dates saw the emergence of several major world religions in Asia: Buddhism in India, Daoism and Confucianism in China, Zoroastrianism in Persia, and Christianity in West Asia. In East Asia the first emperor, Shi Huangdi, united China under the Qin Dynasty at about the same time as Rome began its rise to power, and the armies of the Han Dynasty had expanded Chinese rule into Korea, Central Asia, and Vietnam by the beginning of the 1st millennium A.D. In South Asia the Mauryan kings created an empire in north and central India that lasted for nearly 200 years in the late 1st millennium B.C.; in the 4th century A.D. another Indian dynasty, the Guptas, extended their power through northern India.

On the other side of the globe in Mesomerica the Zapotec civilization flourished for hundreds of years around Monte Alban in Mexico, and the Maya civilization was emerging in the Yucatan peninsula and Guatemala. Their sophisticated cultures developed in isolation from the rest of world; the Mesoamericans built elaborately carved stone pyramids for religious rituals and used a complex and highly complicated astronomical calendar.

ABBREVIATIONS	
mi	miles
cm	centimeters
m	meters
km	kilometers
sq. km	square kilometers
mya	million years ago
c.	about (from the Latin word circa)

A NOTE ON DATES
This set follows standard Western practice in dating events from the start of the Christian era, presumed to have begun in the year 0. Those that happened before the year 0 are listed as B.C. (before the Christian era), and those that happened after as A.D. (from the Latin Anno Domini, meaning "in the year of the Lord"). Wherever possible, exact dates are given; where there is uncertainty, the date is prefixed by the abbreviation c. (short for Latin circa, meaning "about") to show that it is approximate.

ABOUT THIS SET

This book is one of a set of ten providing timelines for world history from the beginning of recorded history up to 2000 A.D. Each volume arranges events that happened around the world within a particular period and is made up of three different types of facing two-page spreads: timelines, features, and glossary pages ("Facts at a Glance," at the back of the book). The three should be used in combination to find the information that you need. Timelines list events that occurred between the dates shown on the pages and cover periods ranging from several centuries at the start of Volume 1, dealing with early times, to six or seven years in Volumes 9 and 10, addressing the modern era.

In part, the difference reflects the fact that much more is known about recent times than about distant eras. Yet it also reflects a real acceleration in the number of noteworthy events, related to surging population growth. Demographers estimate that it was only in the early 19th century that world population reached one billion; at the start of the 21st century the figure is over six billion and rising, meaning that more people have lived in the past 200 years than in all the other epochs of history combined.

The subjects covered by the feature pages may be a major individual or a civilization. Some cover epoch-making events, while others address more general themes such as the development of types of technology. In each case the feature provides a clear overview of its subject to supplement its timeline entries, indicating its significance on the broader canvas of world history.

Facts at a Glance lists names and terms that may be unfamiliar or that deserve more explanation than can be provided in the timeline entries. Check these pages for quick reference on individuals, peoples, battles, or cultures, and also for explanations of words that are not clear.

The comprehensive index at the back of each book covers the entire set and will enable you to follow all references to a given subject across the ten volumes.

TIMELINE PAGES

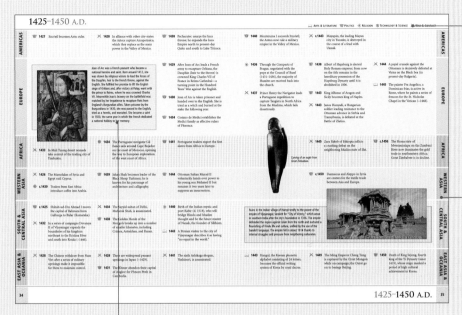

Symbols
Each entry is prefixed by one of five symbols—for example, crossed swords for war, an open book for arts and literature—indicating a particular category of history. A key to the symbols is printed at the top of the right-hand page.

Bands
Each timeline is divided into five or six bands relating to different continents or other major regions of the world. Within each band events are listed in chronological (time) order.

Boxes
Boxes in each timeline present more detailed information about important individuals, places, events, or works.

FEATURE PAGES

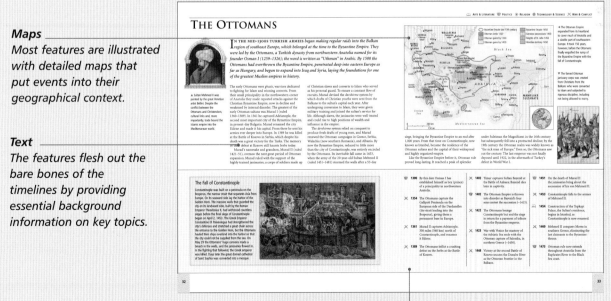

Maps
Most features are illustrated with detailed maps that put events into their geographical context.

Text
The features flesh out the bare bones of the timelines by providing essential background information on key topics.

Subject-specific timelines
Each feature has a timeline devoted exclusively to its topic to give an at-a-glance overview of the main developments in its history.

AMERICAS

c.500 The Zapotec people of the Oaxaca Valley of central Mexico establish a political and ceremonial center at the hilltop site of Monte Albán.

Chavín carving from a temple wall in Peru.

c.500 In Peru the Chavín temple culture, developed from 1200 B.C. on, is still dominant from the edge of the Amazon Basin to the Pacific Coast.

EUROPE

c.500 Ironworking is introduced into Scandinavia.

c.500 Powerful chiefdoms develop in the area between the Rhône, Rhine, and Danube rivers in central Europe; two-wheeled chariots are now in use.

494 The Roman people (plebeians) form an assembly to represent their interests against the aristocrats.

474 The Etruscans are defeated in a naval battle against the city of Cumae in southern Italy.

c.460 The Greek physician Hippocrates, traditionally regarded as the founder of the scientific study of medicine, is born.

457 In Greece war breaks out between the city-states of Athens and Sparta (–445).

451 In Rome the Laws of the Twelve Tables, which extend legal privileges to all Roman citizens, are laid down.

c.450 The Celtic peoples of central Europe begin to develop a style of art known as La Tène (after the site in Switzerland where it was first rediscovered in the 19th century).

AFRICA

c.500 Traders from Saba in Arabia (the biblical land of Sheba, in modern Yemen) found trading settlements on the Red Sea coast of East Africa.

The Nok Culture is named for the village in Nigeria where its artifacts were first discovered in the 1940s. In all, some 150 stylized terracotta heads and figurines have been found. Although the Nok tradition itself died out by about 200 A.D., a sculptural tradition survived in the area: The worldfamous Ife bronzes were produced in the same region more than a millennium later.

WESTERN ASIA

499 The Greek cities of Ionia on the Aegean coast of Asia Minor (modern Turkey) rebel against Persian rule.

490 King Darius of Persia launches an attack against mainland Greece to punish the city-states there for their support of the Ionian cities. His forces are defeated at the Battle of Marathon.

480 Darius's successor, Xerxes I, resumes the attempt to conquer Greece. The Persian invasion force is first temporarily checked at Thermopylae and then suffers a naval defeat at the Battle of Salamis.

479 The Persian invasion force is compelled to withdraw after further defeats at Plataea and Mykale

448 The Peace of Kallias secures the independence of the Ionian cities from Persia.

424 The assassination of King Xerxes II leads to a period of political weakness and disintegration in Persia.

SOUTH & CENTRAL ASIA

c.500 The Sinhalese begin to settle Ceylon (modern Sri Lanka) from India.

c.500 The *Upanishads*, collections of sacred Hindu texts, are written down.

c.500 Magadha, ruled by King Bimbisara, is the most powerful of the Hindu states of northern India.

c.483 Death of Siddhartha Gautama, the Buddha or Enlightened One.

c.480 King Vijaya is reputed to have founded the first state on Ceylon.

EAST ASIA & OCEANIA

c.500 Ironworking begins in Southeast Asia (Vietnam, Cambodia, and Thailand).

c.500 Jin is the most powerful state in Zhou China.

c.500 Sun Tzu writes the *Art of War*, the earliest military handbook.

👑 **c.400** The Olmec civilization of the Gulf Coast is by now in steep decline. Its main ceremonial center at La Venta is demolished at about this time.

⊛ **c.400** At El Mirador, an early Mayan site in the Petén lowlands of southern Mexico, construction begins on the central acropolis (raised earthen mound).

☀ **448** The Athenian statesman Pericles starts construction of the Parthenon, a temple to the goddess Athena completed over the following 10 years under the supervision of the sculptor Phidias.

👑 **c.400** As the Gauls (Celts) begin to cross the Alps and settle in northern and central Italy, Etruscan power goes into decline.

📖 **c.430** The Greek writer Herodotus, regarded as the first historian of the western world, completes his nine-book history of the conflict between Greece and Persia.

⊛ **c.400** The La Tène culture reaches Britain.

The plain of Thermopylae in northern Greece, where Greek forces delayed a Persian army.

⊛ **c.500** The Nok Culture, noted for its striking terracotta sculptures, emerges in northern Nigeria.

⊛ **c.500** Meroë, capital of Nubia, flourishes as an important center of ironmaking.

✕ **480** Carthaginian forces invade Sicily in support of the island's Phoenician colonists, but are defeated by Greek troops.

⊛ **c.470** Carthaginians under Hanno explore the West African coast.

✕ **404** The Egyptians rebel against their Persian rulers, who have governed the country since 525; Egypt becomes more or less independent once again.

👑 **c.420** The Nabateans establish a kingdom in western Arabia, with its capital at Petra in what is now Jordan.

⊛ **410** The earliest surviving horoscope, made by a Babylonian astrologer, dates from this time.

Head of baked clay from the Persian capital, Persepolis, c.450 B.C.

✕ **401** Cyrus, the Persian governor of Anatolia, recruits a Greek army to support a rebellion against his brother, the Emperor Artaxerxes II. After Cyrus's death in battle the Greeks find themselves stranded in the middle of Persia, but fight their way through to the Black Sea and so to safety. The Greeks' fighting retreat is described by their leader, Xenophon, in his classic *Anabasis*.

⊛ **c.450** Reindeer are domesticated by nomadic herders in the Sayan Mountains of Central Asia.

👑 **437** Anuradhapura is founded as the capital of a kingdom in northern Ceylon.

✕ **481** The Warring States Period begins in China, lasting until 221 B.C.; the Zhou realm breaks up amid constant warfare between rival kingdoms.

📖 **479** Death of Confucius (Kongfuzi), the Chinese sage whose name is given to the body of Chinese beliefs known as Confucianism.

AMERICAS

EUROPE

AFRICA

WESTERN ASIA

SOUTH & CENTRAL ASIA

EAST ASIA & OCEANIA

500–400 B.C.

THE GREEK CITY-STATES

A

T THE BEGINNING OF THE 5TH CENTURY B.C. *the Greek world was divided among a number of powerful city-states—independent cities that controlled a surrounding territory of land and had their own system of government. A Greek's first loyalty was to his city, and wars between the city-states were frequent. Nevertheless the Greeks (who called themselves Hellenes) shared many cultural ties, including a common language, system of writing, and religion.*

▲ Of all the Greek city-states Athens, with its democratic tradition, won the greatest fame. The foremost Athenian statesman was Pericles (c.495–429 B.C.), who oversaw the building of the Parthenon temple and steered the city in the time of its greatest prosperity.

By 500 B.C. the two leading city-states in Greece were Sparta and Athens. Sparta was a militaristic state—at age seven boys were taken away from their families and raised as future soldiers. Sparta had used its great military strength to acquire mastery over a large part of the Peloponnese Peninsula of southern Greece.

Athens, situated on the coast near the neck of land leading to the Peloponnese, had grown rich on seaborne trade. It was a democracy, allowing its citizens to vote on important issues such as whether to declare war. However, there were limitations to its democratic franchise: Citizenship was restricted to free men aged at least 20 who were born in Athens and whose parents were Athenians. Women, slaves, and foreigners were excluded.

Some centuries earlier, migrants from Greece had founded a number of city-states along the Aegean coast of Asia Minor (present-day Turkey), an area that the Greeks called Ionia. The Ionian cities had been ruled by Persia since the mid-6th century B.C. When they rebelled in 499 B.C., Athens and other mainland city-states came to their aid. As soon as the Persian King Darius had quelled the uprising, he assembled a huge army and navy to punish the rebels' supporters across the Aegean Sea. In all, the Persians sent three invasion forces to Greece between 492 and 480 B.C., but each time they were driven back by the sheer courage of the much smaller Greek armies pitted against them.

The fear of invasion united Sparta and Athens as never before; but once the Persian threat had

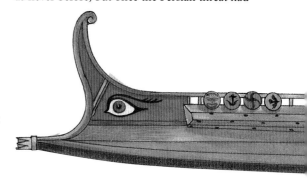

The Classical Age of Greece

Scholars give the name "the Classical Age" to the culture of 5th-century-B.C. Greece, when Greek architecture, literature, art, and science were unsurpassed throughout the Mediterranean world. In the time of Pericles, the politician who dominated Athenian life from 461 to 430 B.C., artists and sculptors adorned the city with magnificent monuments, including the Parthenon (*right*), a temple dedicated to Athene, whose interior was dominated by a huge statue of the goddess. Each year during the festival of Dionysus citizens flocked to the theater to see performances of plays by dramatists such as Aeschylus and Sophocles, while thinkers like Socrates and (in the following century) Plato and Aristotle raised the study of philosophy to new heights.

▶ By the 5th century B.C. the influence of the city-states stretched well beyond the Greek mainland. Greeks had long before settled the west coast of Asia Minor, where they came under the sway of the Persian Empire. Now they also controlled much of southern Italy and Sicily.

▼ When Athenians consulted the Delphic oracle to learn how to face up to the power of Persia, they were told to seek safety in wooden walls. The walls in question turned out to be those of ships like this trireme, so called because it held three banks of rowers. Athens used its fleet first to defeat the Persians at the Battle of Salamis, then to build a maritime empire.

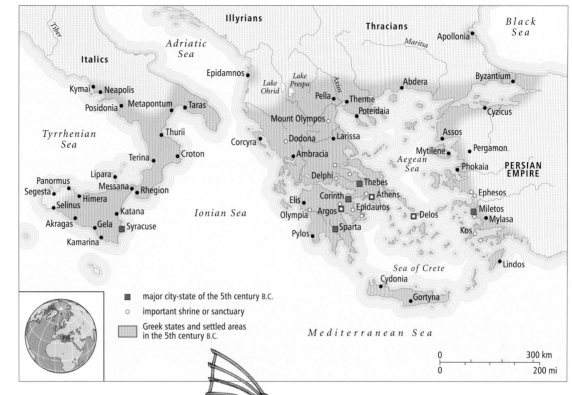

- ■ major city-state of the 5th century B.C.
- ○ important shrine or sanctuary
- Greek states and settled areas in the 5th century B.C.

0   300 km
0   200 mi

disappeared, the old rivalry between the two reemerged stronger than ever. Both Sparta and Athens wanted to dominate Greece, and for the next 75 years their bitter quarrels plunged them and the other Greek city-states into a series of costly conflicts, known as the Peloponnesian Wars. Although Greek culture continued to flourish, the constant strife weakened Greece politically and sapped its economy.

⚔ **490 B.C.** King Darius of Persia invades Greece, but is defeated by an Athenian army at Marathon. A soldier, Pheidippides, runs 24 miles (39 km) to bring news of the victory to Athens; the modern marathon race is named for this feat.

⚔ **480** Spartans fight to the last man in an attempt to halt a fresh Persian invasion at Thermopylae, but fail. The Persians, under Xerxes, overrun Athens, but are turned back after defeat in the naval Battle of Salamis.

⚔ **479** A combined Spartan and Athenian army decisively defeats Xerxes' army at the Battle of Plataea. The Greeks destroy the remnants of the Persian fleet at Mykale, ending further Persian attempts to invade Greece.

👑 **478** Athens makes itself head of an anti-Persian league of Greek cities; Sparta withdraws from the alliance against Persia.

👑 **461** The politician Pericles comes to power in Athens and undertakes a series of reforms.

⚔ **457–445** The First Peloponnesian War breaks out between Athens and Sparta.

📖 **448** The Parthenon—a marble temple dedicated to the goddess Athene—is built as a thanks offering for the Athenian victory over the Persians; Phidias, the greatest sculptor of ancient Greece, carves the great gold and ivory statue of Athena that dominates the temple.

⚔ **431** Hostilities are renewed between Athens and Sparta (the Second Peloponnesian War).

📖 **430** Socrates begins his career as a teacher and philosopher in Athens.

⚔ **416** The Athenians lead an expedition against the island of Sicily, but are forced to withdraw in 413.

⚔ **405** The Spartans defeat the Athenian fleet at Aegospotami, spelling the end of Athens as a major power.

📖 **c. 404–396** The Athenian historian Thucydides writes his masterwork, *The History of the Peloponnesian War*.

AMERICAS

c.370 In southern coastal Peru a new art style—the Nazca—emerges; it features highly colored textiles, mostly tapestries.

Nazca vase decoration featuring stylized hunters and parrots.

c.350 Cities and states develop among the Maya people of Central America.

EUROPE

399 The philosopher Socrates, convicted of corrupting the youth of Athens by his teachings, is forced to drink hemlock, a deadly poison.

396 Rome begins to expand territorially by capturing its northern neighbor, the Etruscan city of Veii.

390 A band of Gauls led by Brennus attacks and occupies the city of Rome for seven months.

c.385 Plato founds the Academy in Athens as a school for teaching philosophy.

371 The city of Thebes defeats Sparta to become the leading city-state in Greece.

348 Rome concludes a nonaggression treaty with the North African city of Carthage, the strongest power in the western Mediterranean.

AFRICA

c.400 Ironworking spreads to the Ethiopian Highlands of East Africa.

380 Nectanebo I seizes the throne of Egypt, starting the nation's 30th and last native dynasty.

343 Persian forces under Artaxerxes III reconquer Egypt.

332 Alexander the Great takes Egypt from Persian control.

331 Alexander founds the city of Alexandria on Egypt's Mediterranean coast.

305 In the power vacuum following Alexander's death Ptolemy, Egypt's Macedonian governor, proclaims himself pharaoh; the Ptolemaic Dynasty that he founds will rule Egypt until 30 B.C.

WESTERN ASIA

358 After a period of unrest Artaxerxes III succeeds to the throne of Persia and reasserts royal authority over the rebellious satraps (governors).

c.350 The widow of King Mausolus of Caria in Asia Minor commissions leading Greek sculptors to build his tomb, the Mausoleum, at Halicarnassus; it becomes one of the Seven Wonders of the Ancient World.

335 Darius III becomes Persia's ruler.

334 Alexander the Great of Macedon invades the Persian Empire.

331 Alexander defeats a Persian army at the Battle of Gaugamela, winning control of Mesopotamia.

SOUTH & CENTRAL ASIA

364 Under the Nanda Dynasty (– 321), the Kingdom of Magadha dominates the Ganges Plain.

c.350 Scythian tribes in the Black Sea area of southern Russia are abandoning nomadism to establish permanent trading settlements on the Dnieper and Don rivers.

329 Alexander the Great conquers Bactria and Sogdiana (modern Afghanistan and Uzbekistan) and invades the Indus Valley (– 326).

EAST ASIA & OCEANIA

c.371 Birth of Mengzi (known in the West as Mencius), Chinese philosopher and moralist in the tradition of Confucius, whose teachings are preserved in the *Book of Mengzi*.

361 Xiao becomes ruler of Qin in western China; his chief minister, Shang Yang, introduces sweeping reforms to end the power of the aristocracy and strengthen the army.

c.350 The crossbow is invented in China.

Chinese warrior with crossbow.

AMERICAS

✳ **c.300** Pottery, introduced to North America from Mexico, is thought to be in use in the Southwest by this time.

☀ **c.300** In Peru the influence of the Chavín Culture has now reached a peak; its style of art and architecture dominates the entire region.

EUROPE

✕ **343** Rome begins a series of wars against its neighbors, the Samnites; by 290 it will emerge as the major power in central Italy.

✕ **338** Philip II of Macedon defeats a Greek army at the Battle of Charonea and wins control of the Greek city-states.

👑 **336** After the murder of Philip II his son Alexander becomes king of Macedon and adopts Philip's plan to invade Persia; he will be known to history as Alexander the Great.

📖 **335** The philosopher Aristotle sets up a school at Athens, the Lyceum.

✳ **c.330** The Greek navigator and geographer Pytheas makes a voyage of exploration in the Atlantic, sailing past Spain, France, and the east coast of Britain to reach a country he calls "Thule," probably northern Norway.

AFRICA

Alexandria on Egypt's Mediterranean coast was one of the chief centers of the Hellenistic (Greek-inspired) culture that spread across the Near and Middle East in the wake of Alexander the Great's conquests. Shown here in a 19th-century print, its library—housed in Ptolemy's Museum—was the finest in the world in its day, and such famous scholars as the mathematician Euclid and the scientist Archimedes studied there.

📖 **c.300** Ptolemy founds the Museum at Alexandria.

WESTERN ASIA

✕ **330** Alexander burns down the Persian royal palace at Persepolis. Darius III is subsequently murdered by one of his own satraps (governors), leaving Alexander in undisputed control of all the Persian Empire's lands.

👑 **323** The death of Alexander the Great unleashes a lengthy power struggle between his successors for control of the lands he conquered.

👑 **305** Seleucus, one of Alexander's former generals, establishes the Seleucid Kingdom in Mesopotamia and Persia.

✕ **301** Seleucus employs war elephants to defeat his rival Antigonos at the Battle of Ipsos in Anatolia.

SOUTH & CENTRAL ASIA

👑 **c.321** Chandragupta Maurya, founder of India's Mauryan Empire, seizes power in Magadha; he reigns until about 297.

✕ **c.311** Chandragupta extends his kingdom as far as the Indus Valley, where he encounters resistance from Alexander's successors.

EAST ASIA & OCEANIA

✕ **c.350** Earthen frontier walls are built in northern China as a defense against invading nomads; they will eventually be linked together to form the Great Wall of China (– 214).

✕ **312** Qin is now the strongest state in China after a series of military campaigns against its neighbors and border nomads.

400–300 B.C.

ALEXANDER THE GREAT

GREEK POWER, PREVIOUSLY LIMITED *to the Mediterranean region, was carried deep into Asia by Alexander the Great, a military genius who ranks among the greatest generals of all time. From the small mountain kingdom of Macedon in northern Greece he set out on a seemingly foolhardy campaign to conquer the vast Persian Empire, a task he in fact accomplished with supreme success. He went on to extend Greek control as far as the borders of India.*

▲ Before setting out to conquer the mighty Persian Empire, Alexander had first to put down a rebellion in mainland Greece, which his father had brought under Macedon's sway. In a ruthless campaign he stormed the city of Thebes, killing 6,000 of its citizens. Thereafter no Greek city dared to openly defy him.

▶ Alexander set out to conquer the Persian Empire, which at the time included both Asia Minor (Turkey) and Egypt, with an army only 35,000 strong. He succeeded in extending his realm as far as the Indus River, founding more than a dozen cities (several of them called Alexandria) along the way.

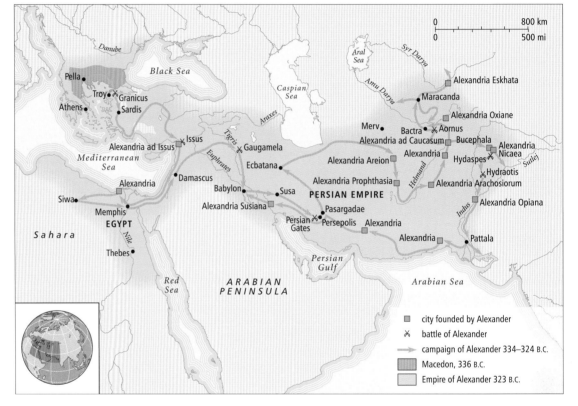

- ■ city founded by Alexander
- ✕ battle of Alexander
- → campaign of Alexander 334–324 B.C.
- Macedon, 336 B.C.
- Empire of Alexander 323 B.C.

👑 **359 B.C.** Philip II comes to power in Macedon and sets about transforming his small kingdom into a major power.

👑 **343** Philip employs the philosopher Aristotle as tutor to his son Alexander.

👑 **336** Philip is murdered at a wedding, and Alexander succeeds to the throne.

✕ **334** Alexander invades Anatolia and routs a Persian army at the Battle of Granicus.

✕ **333** Alexander defeats the Persian ruler Darius III at the Battle of the Issus River in Syria.

👑 **332** Alexander takes control of Egypt, previously under Persian control.

✕ **331** Alexander defeats Darius once more at the Battle of Gaugamela, finally winning control of the Persian Empire.

✕ **330** Alexander burns the palace of Persepolis.

✕ **329–328** Alexander campaigns in Bactria and Sogdiana (Afghanistan and Uzbekistan) to complete his conquest of the Persian Empire.

✕ **327** Alexander crosses the Indus River and wins a battle against an Indian king.

✕ **326** Alexander reaches the Hyphasis River, a tributary of the Indus and the easternmost point of his expedition; an army revolt forces him to give up his plans to conquer India.

Alexander was only 20 years old when he succeeded to the throne of Macedon in 336 B.C., following the brutal murder of his father, Philip II. Philip had made his kingdom the most powerful state in Greece and was on the point of invading the Persian Empire when he was killed.

Alexander wasted little time in putting his father's daring plan into action. In 334 B.C. he invaded and conquered Anatolia (present-day Turkey), which at the time was a Persian province. He met and defeated two of the empire's armies, one of them led by the Persian King Darius III in person, before turning south along the Mediterranean coast to Egypt—also a Persian possession—which he conquered in 332 B.C.

Now Alexander headed into the heart of Darius's empire. He defeated his rival for a second time before entering Persepolis, the capital of the Persian kings, which he burned to the ground. Darius fled and was murdered soon afterward by one of his own satraps (governors), disillusioned by the ruler's military failures. For more than three years the Macedonian army campaigned ceaselessly through Central Asia. They reached the Indus River in present-day Pakistan, and Alexander decided to invade northern India. But his army had had enough, and Alexander was forced to agree to their demands to return home.

Alexander died suddenly in 323 while in Babylon planning his next campaign. His empire immediately collapsed into chaos. His heirs, a mad brother and an infant son, were murdered, and his Macedonian generals, whom he had appointed provincial governors, fought to carve out independent kingdoms for themselves in the lands Alexander had conquered.

While on his campaigns, Alexander founded Greek cities across the lands he conquered, all the way from Alexandria in Egypt to Bactria (in present-day Afghanistan). In his wake the Greek language, together with Greek architecture, sculpture, learning, and cultural pursuits, dominated much of the ancient world for several centuries. Historians call this period the Hellenistic Age (from "Hellene," the word the Greeks used to describe themselves).

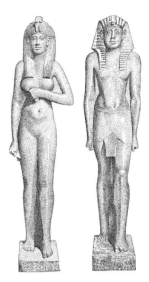

▲ The Ptolemaic Dynasty set up in Egypt after Alexander's death combined Greek and Egyptian traditions in its art.

Alexandria: A Greek City in Egypt

Alexander founded his first city at the mouth of the Nile, naming it Alexandria after himself. Under the Ptolemies, a line of pharaohs descended from Alexander's Macedonian general Ptolemy, Alexandria became the greatest city in the Greek-speaking world. Among the men who made it the foremost center of learning of the Hellenistic Age were Euclid, the father of geometry, the engineer Hero, inventor of a stationary steam engine, and the mathematician Eratosthenes. Best known of Alexandria's monuments was the Pharos, or lighthouse (*right*), one of the Seven Wonders of the Ancient World, which stood 400 feet (120 m) tall at the entrance to the harbor. Today the ruins of the city's ancient center lie offshore under the sea; marine archaeologists are currently investigating them.

⚔ **325–324** After sailing down the Indus River to the coast, Alexander returns to Persia on an overland route across the Baluchistan Desert; his army suffers great losses.

⚔ **323** Alexander dies suddenly in Babylon.

👑 **322** Perdiccas becomes regent on behalf of Alexander's infant son. Ptolemy, one of Alexander's finest generals, seizes control of Egypt.

👑 **321** Perdiccas is murdered by rivals on an expedition to Egypt.

⚔ **320–301** Alexander's empire breaks up as his generals seize territory for themselves in the course of the Wars of the Diadochi ("Wars of the Successors").

👑 **317** Philip III, Alexander's half-brother, is murdered.

👑 **310** Murder of Alexander IV, son of Alexander the Great and last member of the dynasty.

👑 **305** Ptolemy has himself proclaimed pharaoh of Egypt, founding a dynasty (the Ptolemaic) that will rule for 275 years until 30 B.C.

⚔ **301** At the Battle of Ipsos Seleucus establishes his hold over the eastern portion of Alexander's empire, extending the Seleucid Kingdom, which will survive until 63 B.C.

AMERICAS

✳ **c.300** Earliest date proposed for the emergence of the Hohokam Culture in Arizona, with a lifestyle based on the cultivation of corn, beans, cotton, and tobacco.

✳ **c.300** The city of Izapa flourishes in southwestern Mexico: its culture represents an intermediate phase between those of the Olmecs and the Maya.

EUROPE

⚔ **298** The Third Samnite War begins; the Romans' final victory over the Samnites and their Celtic allies eight years later will ensure their dominance over the whole of central Italy (–290).

♛ **287** Rome's plebeians (common people) are accorded equal rights with patricians (nobles).

✳ **287** Archimedes is born in the Greek colony of Syracuse, Sicily: He will be remembered for calculating the value of pi and for breakthroughs in science and mechanics.

⚔ **280** Pyrrhos, king of Epiros, crosses the Adriatic Sea to defend his allies in the Greek cities of southern Italy against the Roman threat.

Roman plate showing a war elephant.

AFRICA

✳ **c.300** Euclid, a Greek mathematician working at the court of Ptolemy I in Alexandria, outlines the main principles of geometry.

✳ **297** Construction begins on Alexandria's Pharos lighthouse, which will become one of the Seven Wonders of the Ancient World.

♛ **285** Ptolemy I gives up his throne as Egypt's pharaoh to his son, Ptolemy II Philadelphus.

WESTERN ASIA

♛ **280** Antiochos I, the son of Alexander the Great's companion Seleucus, inherits the Seleucid Kingdom, made up of Alexander's conquests in Syria, Mesopotamia, and Persia.

♛ **278** Tens of thousands of Celts cross the Dardanelles Strait into Asia Minor. They come as mercenaries, but stay to establish their own state of Galatia in central Anatolia.

⚔ **247** After decades of raiding, Parthian nomads from Central Asia settle down more permanently as rulers of an empire in northern Iran.

⚔ **219** The Seleucid ruler Antiochos III invades the Bible lands, previously a possession of Ptolemaic Egypt. After a bitter struggle he is driven back by the forces of Ptolemy IV.

SOUTH & CENTRAL ASIA

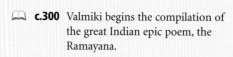

📖 **c.300** Valmiki begins the compilation of the great Indian epic poem, the Ramayana.

Hanuman, the monkey general—a popular character from the Ramayana.

♛ **c.297** Chandragupta Maurya dies, having exploited the chaos following the invasion of Alexander the Great to found an empire extending across the whole of northern India.

EAST ASIA & OCEANIA

✳ **c.300** The Yayoi Culture spreads north and east from western Japan, sustained by systematic rice cultivation and bringing skills in metalworking (both bronze and iron), spinning and weaving, and ceramics.

✳ **c.300** The appearance of a Sanskrit-based alphabet in Cambodia implies the presence of Indian traders in this part of Southeast Asia.

📖 **c.300** The late Ban Chiang Period in Thailand is marked by fine pottery with extravagant swirling and spiraling designs.

Bronze panels from the Yayoi Culture, Japan.

👑 **c.300** With a massive circular pyramid at its heart, Cuicuilco reaches its height as an urban center, dominating the Valley of Mexico, where Mexico City now lies.

⊕ **c.300** Deep shaft tombs are dug in western Mexico at Jalisco, Nayarit, and Colima. Sophisticated ceramic pots and figures are buried with the dead.

☀ **c.300** The city of El Mirador begins to eclipse its Mayan neighbor, Nak'be. Its temple, decorated with giant limestone masks, sets a pattern for later Mayan sites.

AMERICAS

⚔ **279** Celts invade Macedonia and northern Greece.

⚔ **275** Pyrrhos is forced to abandon his campaign against Rome despite considerable military success.

⚔ **264** The First Punic War breaks out between Rome and the North African city of Carthage.

⚔ **241** The First Punic War ends in victory for Rome; Carthage loses its trading colonies in Sicily.

⚔ **218** The Second Punic War begins. The Carthaginian general Hannibal crosses the Alps with a force of 46,000 men and 37 war elephants to invade Italy from the north.

⚔ **216** Hannibal defeats the Romans at the Battle of Cannae.

⚔ **201** At the Battle of Zama Romans led by Scipio Africanus succeed in reversing Hannibal's victory. The Second Punic War ends with Rome in undisputed control of the Mediterranean.

EUROPE

⊕ **c.250** Ironworking reaches sub-Saharan Africa, probably brought across the desert from southern Mauritania to the Niger Valley.

⊕ **240** Eratosthenes, a Greek scholar working in the North African colony of Cyrene, calculates the circumference of the Earth.

AFRICA

From a heartland in central Europe the warlike Celtic peoples spread across much of the continent in the 5th to 3rd centuries B.C. Some headed west into Britain, France, and Spain, others south and east into Italy and the Balkans. From there one group moved on into Asia Minor (Turkey) to found the state of Galatia. This statue of a dying Galatian was sculpted in the Greek city-state of Pergamon.

⚔ **203** Antiochos III's second attempt to take the Bible lands from the Ptolemies is again fiercely resisted (although supported by the local population). By the end of the century he is finally master in Jerusalem.

WESTERN ASIA

👑 **c.269** The Mauryan Empire reaches its height with the accession of Ashoka: In his 37-year reign he will extend his power over all but the far south of the Indian subcontinent.

⚔ **c.261** Ashoka conquers Kalinga, the last outpost of resistance to Mauryan rule.

📖 **c.250** The Sanskrit language, once confined to the northern Indian territories settled by the Aryans, starts to penetrate to southern areas around this time.

SOUTH & CENTRAL ASIA

📖 **c.289** Death of Mengzi, the Chinese philosopher who did more than anyone else to popularize the creed of Confucius.

📖 **c.278** Qu Yuan, widely revered as the father of Chinese poetry, dies. He is believed to have been born around 340 B.C.

⚔ **221** The Warring States Period ends with final victory for the Kingdom of Qin and the unification of China under the First Emperor, Shihuangdi.

👑 **210** Shihuangdi dies and is buried with a "Terracotta Army" of more than 7,000 pottery soldiers.

👑 **206** Traditional date for the foundation of the Kingdom of Nam Viet, located in southern China and what is now northern Vietnam.

👑 **c.200** The first settlers occupy the Marquesas Islands in Polynesia, bringing with them the skills of the Lapita Culture.

EAST ASIA & OCEANIA

CHINA'S FIRST EMPEROR

AS THE 5TH CENTURY B.C. BEGAN, *the vast country we think of as China barely existed: Instead, a score of separate states sparred and jostled for advantage across its lands. In theory all of these states acknowledged the overlordship of the Zhou Dynasty, which had ruled the country since the 11th century B.C.; in practice, however, the Zhou emperors' powers had been in decline for centuries. In the course of the early 3rd century B.C., however, one kingdom succeeded in forcing its dogged way to military and political supremacy. The triumph of Qin represented the historic birth of imperial China.*

▲ The Great Wall of China had its origins in a series of earthworks built from the 4th century B.C. on to defend the nation's northern borders against nomadic tribesmen. The First Emperor linked these fortifications together into a single earth-and-masonry defensive line. Much of the wall was subsequently rebuilt in later times.

The Terracotta Army

Shihuangdi's burial mound rises high above the fields near the city of Xian in central China; it has yet to be excavated, but ancient sources suggest that a fabulous complex of passages and chambers lies within it. Legend has it that 700,000 prisoners labored for years to throw up this extraordinary earthwork. Equally astonishing, however, are the treasures uncovered in three pits found about a mile (1.6 km) away. Here, concealed in wood-roofed vaults, stands an army of lifesize terracotta figures 7,000 strong, lined up in defense of their dead commander-in-chief to serve as his bodyguards in the afterlife. The force includes officers and generals as well as ordinary soldiers armed with spears; there are mounted cavalrymen and charioteers as well as crossbowmen. Each is an individual: No two faces are the same, and a wide range of ages, physiques, and characters is represented.

👑 **481 B.C.** The "Warring States" Period begins: A weakened China is divided among about 20 different kingdoms vying for supremacy. In theory the emperors of the Eastern Zhou Dynasty still have overall control, but in practice their authority counts for little.

👑 **361** The philosopher Shang Yang becomes chief minister of the Kingdom of Qin, at the time a small realm in western China. Over the next 21 years he turns it into a strong, centralized state.

⚔ **314** The Kingdom of Qin wins a victory over nomads from the north, marking its emergence as a new military power in western China.

👑 **312** The Ba and Shu kingdoms of northern Sichuan, as well as parts of the Han Kingdom to the east, fall under Qin dominance.

👑 **c.280** By this date the conflicts of the Warring States are slowly drawing toward a resolution: Only six main kingdoms—Qin, Zhao, Wei, Han, Chu, and Zhou—now survive as independent states.

👑 **259** The Kingdom of Qin defeats its main rival, Zhao. The remaining states are subjugated in the decades that follow.

👑 **258** Ying Sheng, the future First Emperor, is born.

⚔ **256** The Qin army defeats forces loyal to the last Zhou emperor, forcing him to abdicate (give up power).

👑 **246** At the age of 12 Ying Sheng succeeds his father, Zhuang Xiang, as ruler of the Kingdom of Qin.

Qin used to be transliterated as "Ch'in," from which comes our word "China": It is fitting that this state should have given the modern country its name. Less just is the way Westerners have let the name of Qin's mightiest ruler be forgotten, for few historic figures have towered so imposingly as Ying Sheng, who united China under Qin rule. Born in 258 B.C., the son of Xiao Wen, the ruler of Qin, Ying Sheng was raised at a time when the conflicts of China's Warring States Period were heading toward resolution. Of the crowd of petty kingdoms that had once vied for supremacy, only a handful remained, among which Qin's ascendancy was becoming clear.

The way had been well prepared for the reunification of China, which took place early in Ying Sheng's reign. He then set about shaping his conquests into a coherent whole. In 221 he formalized the unification of all the former kingdoms into a single gigantic state, a feat that subsequently earned him the title of Shihuangdi, or First Emperor.

With the determination of a visionary and the brutality of a despot, he then launched an extraordinary program of nationbuilding. First, he took possession of his empire, disarming local warlords and subjecting them to his rule; for administrative purposes he divided his realm into 36 provinces, each overseen by officials answering to him. A network of new roads and canals improved communications. To encourage trade, weights and measures were standardized across China, as was the width of wagon axles, so all carts could trundle along the same road ruts. All the emperor's dominions had to accept a single, harsh legal code; he also took steps to reform the Chinese written language so as to make it understandable to all his subjects.

More sinister, to modern eyes, was Shihuangdi's concern to police his people's minds. Fearing the disruptive effect of philosophical arguments on his newly united realm, he had books burned in their

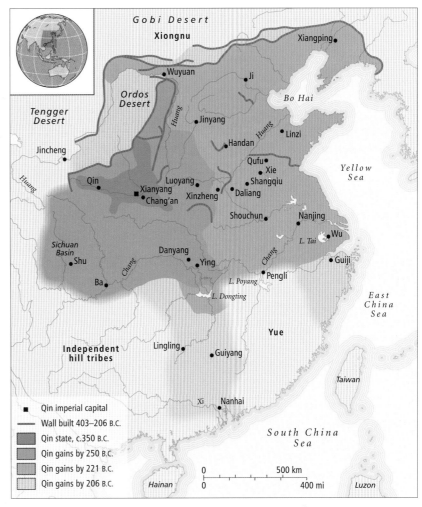

thousands at public ceremonies and also reportedly had some 400 dissident scholars killed. Opponents of his rule were treated mercilessly. Yet, tyrant that he was, Shihuangdi forced a great nation into being; without him imperial China would never have survived, as it did, for over 2,000 years.

▲ Between 350 and 206 the Qin state expanded from its heartland near the upper reaches of the Huang (Yellow) River to take over much of the area of modern-day China.

Map legend:
■ Qin imperial capital
— Wall built 403–206 B.C.
Qin state, c.350 B.C.
Qin gains by 250 B.C.
Qin gains by 221 B.C.
Qin gains by 206 B.C.

👑 **221** Ying Sheng confers on himself the title of Huangdi, or emperor, of a newly unified China; historians after his death will call him Shihuangdi, or "First Emperor."

👑 **219** Shihuangdi tours his empire, underlining his determination to rule China as a whole.

👑 **214** The Great Wall of China is completed.

⚔ **213** Shihuangdi sends out a military force against the nomads of Xiongnu to the northwest.

👑 **213** When several scholars criticize the emperor's centralizing policies, an increasingly despotic Shihuangdi responds by ordering a series of public book burnings aimed at destroying "useless books."

👑 **212** On the emperor's orders 460 scholars are buried alive for "throwing the common people into confusion."

👑 **210** Shihuangdi dies. On his death civil war breaks out among his heirs.

👑 **206** The entire Qin royal family is massacred by rebels led by a peasant warrior, Liu Bang.

👑 **202** Liu Bang establishes a new dynasty, the Han, becoming its first emperor under the name of Gaozu.

👑 **220 A.D.** The last Han emperor is deposed, and China splits into three kingdoms.

200–100 B.C.

A stele from Monte Albán displays glyphs (characters) of an early Zapotec text.

AMERICAS

☀ **c.200** By this date the influence of Peru's Chavín Culture is in marked decline.

⊛ **c.200** Defensive ramparts are built at Monte Albán in southern Mexico; massive carvings are inscribed with an early Zapotec text.

☀ **c.200** A sacred complex is built at El Mirador, with three temples clustered together on a single platform mound.

EUROPE

👑 **197** Hispania (Spain) becomes a province of the Roman Empire.

⊛ **c.150** The Romans revolutionize engineering and construction with the discovery of how to make and work with concrete.

✕ **149** The Third Punic War begins.

✕ **146** Corinth, leader of the Achaean League, is sacked, effectively bringing Greek resistance to Roman rule to an end.

✕ **146** The Third Punic War comes to an end with the final destruction of Carthage, leaving Rome as the unchallenged master of the Mediterranean Sea.

AFRICA

⊛ **c.200** The Nok Culture reaches its height in central Nigeria.

⊛ **196** Texts celebrating Pharaoh Ptolemy V are carved on the Rosetta Stone in Greek and Egyptian scripts; 2,000 years later they will be the key to deciphering hieroglyphics.

👑 **168** Rome intervenes in a dispute between the Seleucid Kingdom and Ptolemaic Egypt, signaling growing Roman influence in the land of the pharaohs.

WESTERN ASIA

✕ **191** The Seleucid army of Antiochos III the Great is defeated by the Romans at Thermopylae in northern Greece.

✕ **190** A Roman navy defeats the Seleucid fleet off Crete, leaving the way clear for the conquest of Asia Minor; Roman power is confirmed by a crushing land victory over Antiochos's army at Magnesia.

👑 **171** Mithradates I becomes king of the Parthians: By his death in 138 he will have built an empire extending from Afghanistan to the Euphrates River.

☀ **167** Antiochos IV Epiphanes ("God Manifest") outlaws the practice of Judaism even in Judah itself, rededicating the Temple of Jerusalem to the Greek god Zeus. His actions spark off the Revolt of the Maccabeans (followers of Judas Maccabeus).

SOUTH & CENTRAL ASIA

✕ **c.185** Pushyamitra assassinates the last Mauryan emperor in front of his troops to seize power for himself and his successors of the Shunga Dynasty, restoring Hindu rule in India.

2nd-century-B.C. coin from Bactria (in modern Afghanistan) bears Greek inscriptions.

✕ **c.183** Nomadic raiders from Central Asia attack India's northern frontier. So too do the forces of Demetrius, Greek king of Bactria, who establish a foothold in the valleys of northwestern India.

EAST ASIA & OCEANIA

⊛ **c.200** The Sohano Period begins in the Solomon Islands: Its craftspeople make fine pottery decorated with geometric forms.

⊛ **c.200** The water buffalo is used as a draft animal in Southeast Asia from around this time.

👑 **141** Wudi becomes emperor of China: He undertakes a series of military campaigns against nomadic Xiongnu raiders and extends the Great Wall west to the Tarim Basin.

AMERICAS

⊕ **c.200** Development starts on the North Acropolis at Tikal, Guatemala, with the construction of a massive stone platform that will subsequently provide a foundation for several Mayan pyramid temples.

⊕ **c.200** Excavated villages suggest an agrarian lifestyle is being adopted in the region known as Greater Chiriquí, incorporating southern Costa Rica and northern Panama.

👑 **c.150** The eruption of Mt. Xitle devastates Cuicuilco, forcing surviving residents to abandon the city in Mexico.

☀ **c.100** Fine necklaces and other jewelry, made from green, semiprecious stone such as jadeite, are buried with the dead in tombs in parts of Costa Rica.

EUROPE

✕ **133** In Rome, Tiberius Gracchus, Tribune of the People, is assassinated—a dangerous escalation in the longstanding power struggle between the popular Assembly and the aristocratic Senate.

✕ **133** Celtiberian rebels against Roman rule are starved into submission by Scipio Aemilianus after a 15-month siege: The victory marks a shift toward a more aggressive imperial policy.

⊕ **125** Death of Hipparchos (born c.180), the first man to fix location by calculating latitude and longitude.

✕ **102** Uprisings by the Germanic Cimbri and Teutones tribes are ruthlessly put down by the Romans (– 101).

AFRICA

✕ **146** Carthage is laid waste by the forces of Rome.

✕ **104** Jugurtha, ruler of Numidia (in modern Algeria), dies in prison after an unsuccessful rebellion against Roman rule.

WESTERN ASIA

A 19th-century engraving shows Judas Maccabeus inciting the Jews to revolt.

✕ **164** The Maccabeans prevail in Jerusalem; Antiochos is forced to rescind his law, and Judas is left in charge of what will in time emerge as an independent Jewish state (–142).

✕ **141** Mithridates I defeats and captures the Seleucid ruler Demetrius Nicator, ending Seleucid rule in Persia and Mesopotamia.

👑 **133** King Attalos III of Pergamon (in modern Turkey) bequeaths his kingdom to the Romans upon his death; it is soon absorbed into the Roman province of Asia.

SOUTH & CENTRAL ASIA

✕ **c.150** Menander, the most celebrated of the Indo-Greek kings, assassinates his predecessor Eucratides to take control of Bactria; he leads an army of conquest across northern India.

👑 **c.141** The Chinese Emperor Wudi's actions against Xiongnu nomads have repercussions well to the west, pushing Kushan and Saka steppe nomads southward into northern India.

👑 **138** Wudi sends embassies westward in the hope of establishing alliances against the Xiongnu, thereby helping to open up the Silk Road linking China to western Asia and Europe.

EAST ASIA & OCEANIA

👑 **117** In China iron and salt are made state monopolies, increasing the Han Dynasty's control over the nation's economic life.

⊕ **112** The minting of coins is made a state monopoly in Han China.

👑 **111** Wudi's armies conquer the Kingdom of Nam Viet, completing the conquest of southern China and bringing part of today's Vietnam under Chinese control.

✕ **108** Wudi annexes northern Korea.

⊕ **105** Traditional date for the invention of paper, made from scraps of cloth and wood chips, in China. For the next two centuries paper will only be used for wrapping and packing, not for writing.

200–100 B.C.

THE GROWTH OF BUDDHISM

▲ For the first four centuries of the Buddhist era representations of the Buddha were discouraged; it was only in the 2nd century A.D. that the earliest images began to appear. This statue comes from medieval Japan.

DESTINED FOR GREATNESS, *according to the soothsayers, the young prince was kept in isolation from the ills of the world, the pampered prisoner of the palace where he lived with his beautiful wife, the Princess Yasodhara, and their small child. Yet, his curiosity growing, he stole out alone into the city and was shocked by some of the sights that met his eyes. He saw signs of suffering and sickness, old age and mortality— and, most moving of all, a holy man who had chosen a life of simplicity.*

The young man's name was Siddhartha Gautama, and he had been born in the Himalayan foothills of northern India. Leaving his home and family to wander as a beggar, he spent six years in poverty and hunger, yet his sacrifices brought no spiritual return. Realizing that to find enlightenment he would have to start looking inside himself, he sat down beneath a tree, resolved not to move until he had attained a state of spiritual ecstasy. The forces of evil thundered and hurled down lightning bolts, but, transformed by his peaceful presence, they fell as blossoms. Three nights later, his struggles over, Siddhartha stood up and resumed his journey: The bodhisattva (holy man) had become the Buddha.

For over 40 years he wandered through northern India spreading the injunction "Cease to do evil; learn to do good, and purify your heart." Like other Indian thinkers of his time, he believed the dead were reincarnated innumerable times in different human— or even animal—forms, rising or falling in status according to how well they had lived their previous lives. Only when the sacred state of *bodhi* (enlightenment) had been reached could an

individual hope to transcend the swirling cycles of death and rebirth known as *samsara,* and find the final peace he himself had attained as the Buddha.

Simple as the Buddha's message sounded, it was open to endless differences of interpretation; and no sooner had he died, than his followers fell out among themselves. The gravest of many splits would come in the 3rd century B.C., when the Theravada ("Doctrine of the Elders") and Mahayana ("Greater Vehicle") schools separated. Theravada Buddhism emphasized the search for individual enlightenment as outlined by the Buddha in his doctrine of the Eightfold Path: right thinking, right aspiration, right speech, right conduct, right lifestyle, right effort, right mindfulness, and right meditation. Mahayana Buddhism was an altogether more popular faith, encouraging the worship of bodhisattvas—Buddhist saints who had delayed their own attainment of *nirvana*, or release from suffering, to help others do so.

Despite the Buddha's best efforts, his religion remained a minority creed until about 259 B.C., when it was taken up by Ashoka, India's Mauryan ruler, thus becoming the official religion throughout most of

---

※ **483 B.C.** Siddhartha Gautama, the Buddha, dies. The First Great Council of his followers is held to agree on the main tenets of his teaching.

※ **c.383** Said to have been held about a century after the Buddha's death, the Second Great Council concerns itself with details of ritual observance and monastic practice.

※ **c.259** Buddhism finds its most influential convert when the Indian Emperor Ashoka becomes an adherent. His emissaries carry the creed not only across India but beyond, to Sri Lanka and into Southeast Asia.

※ **c.250** Ashoka presides over the Third Great Council at Pataliputra, where doctrinal divisions arise, and the basic tenets of the Theravada tradition are established.

※ **c.185** Buddhism in India suffers a major setback when Pushyamitra seizes power from Ashoka's Mauryan successors: Under the new Shunga Dynasty the Brahmin elite of Hinduism returns to power.

📖 **c.1 A.D.** The *Tripitaka* ("Three Baskets"), or Pali Canon—the nearest thing Theravada Buddhism has to a scripture—is thought to have been completed by about now.

※ **c.50** Brought by Indian merchants and missionaries, Buddhism establishes a presence in China, but makes headway only slowly against the country's own strong spiritual traditions.

※ **c.100** The main elements of Mahayana Buddhism are upheld at a council called by the Kushan ruler Kanishka in Kashmir.

※ **c.200** The *Jatakamala*—a set of stories describing the different former lives of the Buddha—is said to have been written around now by the (perhaps legendary) Aryasura.

The Mountain of Life

The universe, according to Buddhist tradition, rises like a mountain from an endless plain, its sides curving gently upward toward a distant summit. Beneath the ground at its base lie 136 distinct hells where different sins are punished; on the slopes above, the souls of mortals find varying degrees of happiness. The purer the spirit, the higher the place, until, at the mountain's peak, lies the zone of *nirvana* in which the most blessed transcend selfhood and all time. This scheme finds symbolic representation in the lovingly sculpted form of the stupa—a domelike monument of a sort found throughout the Buddhist world. This example (*far right*) is enclosed in a rock-cut temple at Karli in western India.

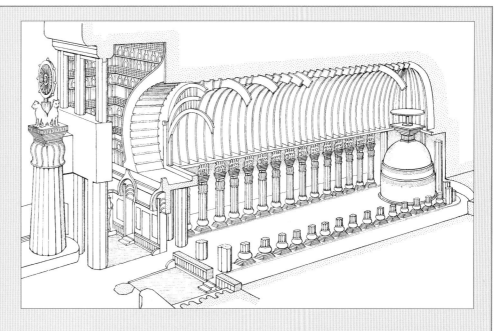

mainland India. Ashoka also sent out missionaries to the island of Sri Lanka and overland to Southeast Asia. In time, missionaries would set out from these places in their turn to preach Buddhism in China, Korea, Japan, and Indonesia. The message would prove more enduring in these far-flung lands than in its Indian birthplace, where, in the years after Ashoka's death, the Hindu Shunga Dynasty worked hard to suppress the upstart faith.

▶ Buddhism's original heartland lay in the prosperous Indian state of Magadha, in the Ganges Valley. Its spread owed much to the Emperor Ashoka, who became a convert around 259 B.C.

☀ **c.367** The first Buddhist missions are established in Tibet.

☀ **372** Missionaries bring Buddhism to Korea, where it will become the state religion for over a millennium.

☀ **c.470** Birth of Bodhidharma, who as a young missionary travels from his native India to China; there he is credited with founding the Chan sect of Buddhism, better known in its later Japanese form as Zen.

☀ **552** Buddhism is introduced from Korea to the Japanese court.

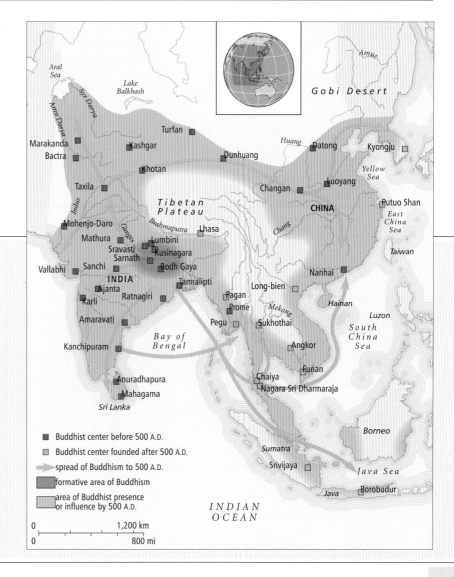

■ Buddhist center before 500 A.D.
□ Buddhist center founded after 500 A.D.
➡ spread of Buddhism to 500 A.D.
▨ formative area of Buddhism
▨ area of Buddhist presence or influence by 500 A.D.

0   1,200 km
0   800 mi

AMERICAS

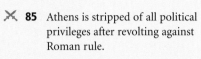

c.100 The Hopewell Culture emerges in the Ohio Valley, extending gradually along the Illinois and Mississippi rivers. A development of the Adena Culture, its ritual life centers on burial mounds.

c.100 Maya nobles at Kaminaljuyú (within modern Guatemala City) are buried with sacrificial attendants and grave goods of jade, obsidian, and mica.

EUROPE

85 Athens is stripped of all political privileges after revolting against Roman rule.

c.80 The Greeks invent a calculator for astronomical or calendrical purposes that uses an elaborate system of intermeshing gears.

Julius Caesar was the greatest general that republican Rome produced, and he was also a talented writer and politician. He used his conquest of Gaul (France) to build up a military power base. When summoned back to Rome by a Senate nervous about his growing ambitions, he came at the head of an army, triggering a civil war that he finally won. However, his rise aroused deep hostility, and he was eventually assassinated by republican conspirators in 44 B.C.

AFRICA

c.100 Alexandria, on the Mediterranean coast of Egypt, produces Greek-style mosaics and frescoes that are eagerly copied in wealthy Roman homes.

51 Cleopatra becomes ruler of Egypt as coregent with her brother. The two become involved in a power struggle that Cleopatra wins with the help of the visiting Julius Caesar (–48).

45 Carthage, destroyed by the Romans a century earlier, is refounded as a Roman city.

WESTERN ASIA

64 The Roman general Pompey conquers Syria.

63 Pompey wins control of the Bible lands for Rome, making Judea part of the province of Syria.

53 The Parthians inflict a humiliating defeat on a Roman army at Carrhae (Haran, in what is now southeast Turkey). Their victory gives them control of the Silk Road, the main trade route between China and the West.

c.50 The invention of glassblowing in Syria revolutionizes the glassmaking industry.

40 Herod the Great is appointed king of Judea by the Roman Senate. He builds a new temple in Jerusalem.

c.10 Using concrete blocks, Herod constructs the first large harbor in the open sea, at Caesarea.

SOUTH & CENTRAL ASIA

c.100 The Silk Road trade route between China and the West across Central Asia is in full swing by this time.

The Silk Road winds through what is now Xinjiang Province, China.

EAST ASIA & OCEANIA

c.90 Sima Qian (c.145–80 B.C.) produces an official Chinese history that becomes a model for government-sponsored histories until modern times.

c.85 The earliest known Chinese lacquerware dates from this time.

52 Chinese astronomer Ken Shou-Ch'ang builds an armillary ring, a metal circle that represents the equator and is used in observing stars.

👑 **c.50** El Mirador in Guatemala develops into the largest lowland Mayan center, covering more than 6 square miles (10 sq. km).

⊛ **36** The earliest Mayan date yet identified is carved on a stele at Chiapa de Corzo in southern Mexico. It corresponds to December 8, 36 B.C.

AMERICAS

⊛ **63** A freed slave employed by the Roman orator Cicero invents a Latin shorthand system.

👑 **60** Rome founds colonies in Switzerland.

✕ **58** Julius Caesar begins a 10-year campaign to conquer Gaul (France).

✕ **55** Julius Caesar briefly invades Britain on what amounts to a military reconnaissance trip.

✕ **54** Julius Caesar returns to Britain and defeats a British army, but then returns to Gaul.

⊛ **46** Julius Caesar introduces the Julian calendar of three 365-day years followed by one of 366 days.

✕ **44** Julius Caesar is assassinated on his way to a meeting of the Roman Senate.

✕ **31** Caesar's heir Octavian triumphs over his rival Mark Antony in the civil war following Caesar's death.

👑 **27** Octavian takes the title Augustus, inaugurating the imperial period of Roman history.

EUROPE

📖 **40** Mark Antony gives Cleopatra 200,000 volumes from the library at Pergamon to add to Ptolemy I's collection in Alexandria, making the latter the greatest in the world.

✕ **31** Octavian's navy, under the command of Agrippa, defeats Antony and Cleopatra's forces at the Battle of Actium.

👑 **30** Antony and Cleopatra commit suicide. Rome annexes Egypt.

AFRICA

The Bible lands had been a Roman province for 23 years when Herod the Great was chosen to rule them in 40 B.C. Although a client of Rome, he was an ambitious monarch, noted for his building work. The site of the Herodium, a fortified palace atop an artificial mound, can still be seen near Jerusalem today (*left*).

☀ **4** Probable year of birth of Jesus Christ in Bethlehem, Judea.

WESTERN ASIA

☀ **c.100** The Great Stupa, a Buddhist monument at Sanchi, India, is doubled in size and clad in lavishly carved stone.

☀ **c.100** A new form of Buddhism, called Mahayana ("Great Vehicle"), starts to take shape. It offers salvation through the help of bodhisattvas—humans who delay the attainment of enlightenment in order to help others.

⊛ **c.50** The *Ayurveda*, a Hindu medical treatise, establishes a holistic medical system that is still practiced today.

SOUTH & CENTRAL ASIA

⊛ **28** Chinese imperial histories begin recording sunspots—dark patches that appear periodically on the sun's surface.

⊛ **c.10** The Chinese invent methods for drilling wells over 3,250 feet (1,000 m) deep to obtain water and natural gas.

EAST ASIA & OCEANIA

100–0 B.C.

THE RISE OF ROME

IN 500 B.C. ROME WAS A TINY *republic hemmed in by other Latin tribes and more advanced Etruscan and Greek city-states. Over the next 250 years it succeeded in dominating Italy by conquest, colonization, or alliance. Victories over Carthage then made it the chief Mediterranean power. But as Rome's overseas territories grew, unrest at home led to dictatorship, civil war, and the replacement of the republican political system by imperial rule.*

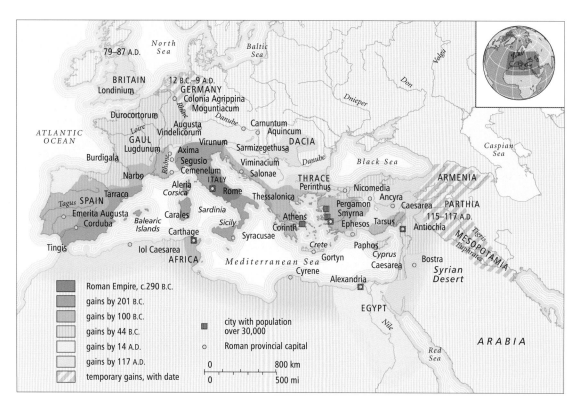

▲ According to legend, Rome was founded by Romulus, who as a child was abandoned with his twin, Remus; the two only survived because a she-wolf suckled them. This bronze statue illustrating the story dates from c.500 B.C., although the twins were added later.

◀ Roman power expanded steadily from the area around Rome itself to take in first Italy and eastern Spain, and then the Mediterranean empire of its defeated rival Carthage. Julius Caesar added Gaul (France) and Germany up to the Rhine frontier. Other territories in Europe, Africa, and Asia followed under the early emperors.

Map legend:
- Roman Empire, c.290 B.C.
- gains by 201 B.C.
- gains by 100 B.C.
- gains by 44 B.C.
- gains by 14 A.D.
- gains by 117 A.D.
- temporary gains, with date
- ■ city with population over 30,000
- ○ Roman provincial capital

0 — 800 km
0 — 500 mi

---

494 B.C. After going on military strike, Roman plebeians (commoners) win the right to appoint tribunes to protect their interests.

451 A code of laws known as the Twelve Tables is drawn up; it defines the rights and obligations of Roman citizens.

312 The first major Roman road, the Appian Way, is begun. Running south from Rome to Capua, it is the first link in a network that will eventually stretch over 50,000 miles (85,000 km).

287 A law (the *Lex Hortensia*) makes resolutions passed in the plebeian assembly binding on all Romans.

275 Victory against an invading army led by King Pyrrhos of Epiros (a Greek kingdom) confirms Rome's mastery over all of Italy.

241 Victory in the First Punic War (264–241) between Rome and Carthage gives Rome control of Sicily, its first overseas province.

218 Hannibal of Carthage starts the Second Punic War (218–201) by invading Italy across the Alps.

203 Despite having inflicted crushing defeats on Roman armies, Hannibal, having failed to take Rome itself, is eventually recalled to Africa.

146 The Third Punic War (149–146) ends with the destruction of Carthage. The province of Africa is founded.

88 After a conflict known as the Social War Rome is forced to grant citizenship to all Italians.

82 Lucius Sulla is appointed dictator of Rome. He butchers his opponents.

In the myths Aeneas, founder of the Roman race, was a prince of Troy, a city famed in Greek legend. In fact, the ancestors of the Romans were immigrants from north of the Alps who spoke the language that was later to develop into Latin. They moved into central Italy in about 1000 B.C. and built villages on hills overlooking the Tiber River. By the 8th century the settlements had merged into the town of Rome.

Early Rome was ruled by kings, including three Etruscan monarchs. Having expelled its last Etruscan ruler, Rome declared itself a republic in 509 B.C. From that time on the state was governed by two elected officials, called consuls, and by the Senate, which drew its membership from the ranks of aristocrats known as patricians. The commoners, or plebeians, in time set up their own assembly and elected officials called tribunes to protect their interests.

The new republic gradually imposed its power over the other Italian states by a combination of military force and diplomacy. Conquered rivals were offered alliances and given privileges, which in some cases included Roman citizenship. In return, the allies had to pay taxes and provide soldiers to serve in the Roman army. The Romans also consolidated their hold on Italy by founding colonies linked by a well-maintained network of roads.

Alliances with Greek cities in southern Italy brought Rome into conflict with Carthage, a trading city on the North African coast. In three campaigns known as the Punic Wars (from the Latin *Punicus*, or "Phoenician," the nationality of Carthage's founders), Rome first achieved naval supremacy, then survived an invasion by the Carthaginian general Hannibal, and finally (in 146 B.C.) destroyed Carthage itself.

The defeat of Carthage opened the way for more Roman conquests. Greece, Asia Minor, Syria, Palestine, and Gaul (modern-day France) all fell to its generals. At home, though, the republican political system was breaking down. The patricians used their wealth to create large country estates worked by slaves. Landless peasants flocked to the cities or joined the army, where they provided the power base for a series of military dictators: Lucius Sulla, Pompey the Great, and Julius Caesar.

After Caesar was murdered by patricians jealous of his power in 44 B.C., civil war broke out between his adopted son, Octavian, and Mark Antony, who planned to create a separate empire with Cleopatra, queen of Egypt. The defeat of Mark Antony's navy at Actium left Octavian as sole ruler of the Roman world. His new title "Augustus," meaning "revered one," would be used by Roman emperors for the next five centuries.

The Roman Army

Rome's well-disciplined citizens' army was a key factor in the early successes of the republic. All property-owning citizens between 17 and 46 could be called up. Soldiers were grouped into infantry units called legions, each of about 4,200 men. In battle a legion was organized in three ranks. Young men armed with thrusting spears and swords formed the first rank. Behind them were older men with better weapons and armor. A reserve of veterans made up the third rank. The poorest soldiers, who could not afford decent weapons, fought as skirmishers. In time the conscript army came to seem unwieldy, and from 104 B.C. on it was replaced by a professional standing force.

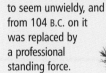

👑 **71** A slave revolt led by a Thracian gladiator named Spartacus is crushed.

👑 **59** The Roman general and politician Pompey the Great forms an illegal alliance with Marcus Crassus and Julius Caesar, intended to further the trio's political ambitions.

⚔ **58–50** In a series of brilliant campaigns Caesar conquers Gaul and raids Britain and the German lands.

⚔ **53** Crassus is defeated and killed by Parthians at the Battle of Carrhae.

⚔ **49** Julius Caesar takes his troops without permission across the Rubicon, a stream separating Italy from Gaul. He fights a civil war with the armies of Pompey.

👑 **45** Following the defeat and death of Pompey, Caesar becomes sole ruler.

👑 **44** Declared dictator for life, Julius Caesar is assassinated by colleagues unwilling to accept one-man rule.

👑 **43** Caesar's adopted son and heir Octavian joins forces with Mark Antony and Marcus Lepidus to reconstitute the government.

👑 **37** Mark Antony, who is married to Octavian's sister, provokes anger in Rome by flaunting his relationship with Cleopatra, queen of Egypt.

⚔ **31** The defeat of Antony and Cleopatra's forces at the naval Battle of Actium leaves Octavian master of the Roman world.

👑 **30** Antony and Cleopatra commit suicide.

👑 **27** Octavian assumes the name Augustus and is given overriding authority over all Rome's territories.

AMERICAS

✳ **c.0** The first "Basketmaker" phase of the Anasazi Culture gets under way in the American Southwest; its economy is based on settled agriculture and on hunting large animals with spearthrowers.

The Pueblo peoples of the American Southwest have one of the continent's oldest cultural traditions. Its deepest roots lie in the Basketmaker Culture, named for the neatly woven baskets that were its most distinctive products. Around 500 A.D. the Basketmaker people started making pottery and living in sunken pithouses—distinctive features of the ensuing Anasazi Culture.

EUROPE

✳ **c.0** The Greek geographer Strabo publishes a detailed description of the known world.

✗ **9** Three Roman legions are wiped out by German tribes in the Teutoburg Forest, north of the Rhine River, which becomes the imperial frontier in Germany.

✗ **43** A Roman army under Claudius conquers Britain and establishes the city of London on the Thames River.

♕ **50** Cologne on the Rhine in Germany becomes a Roman colony.

AFRICA

☀ **c.0** Egyptian-style temples dedicated to the lion god Apedemek are built at Naga in Nubia.

♕ **42** Mauretania (made up of coastal regions of modern Morocco and Algeria) is annexed by Rome.

♕ **c.50** The Greek-influenced Kingdom of Axum is established in Ethiopia and dominates the Red Sea trade in incense.

WESTERN ASIA

♕ **6** Rome annexes Judea as a province of the empire; one of its governors, Pontius Pilate, will later convict Jesus of sedition.

☀ **c.30** Jesus of Nazareth, founder of Christianity, is crucified in Jerusalem.

Roman coin showing Judea in bondage.

♕ **53** Tiridates I founds a line of Armenian kings that lasts for several centuries.

☀ **c.68** A Jewish sect hides more than 600 religious manuscripts in caves at Qumran, Jordan. Discovered in 1947 and known as the Dead Sea Scrolls, the documents include the earliest known copies of the Old Testament.

SOUTH & CENTRAL ASIA

✳ **c.0** Romans establish trading links with southern India, using the monsoon wind system for rapid sea travel.

♕ **c.50** The Kushans, a people from Central Asia, gain control of northwest India, establishing a cosmopolitan empire that lasts for over 300 years.

♕ **c.60** Indian exports of spices, jewels, and textiles become such a drain on the Roman economy that the Emperor Nero bans the import of pepper.

EAST ASIA & OCEANIA

✳ **2** A census gives the population of China's Han Empire as 57 million.

♕ **9** Wang Mang seizes the Chinese throne and introduces radical reforms, including reallocation of land to peasants and restrictions on slave ownership.

✳ **c.10** The Chinese build cast-iron suspension bridges strong enough to carry vehicles.

✗ **25** Wang Mang is assassinated by Han princes who found the Later Han Dynasty.

✗ **c.39** Chinese control of northern Vietnam is challenged by a rebellion led by two sisters, who rule as queens of an independent state before their defeat in c.42.

👑 **c.0** Teotihuacán starts to emerge in the Valley of Mexico, replacing Cuicuilco as the region's main urban center.

☀ **c.0** The Moche people, inhabiting river valleys on the coast of northern Peru, emerge as a significant presence in a region previously dominated by the Chavín Culture.

☀ **c.50** In the desert 300 miles (500 km) south of the Moche lands Peru's Nazca people create vast line drawings that only take on recognizable form when seen from a great height.

👑 **c.50** El Mirador, the largest lowland Mayan city, goes into decline.

☀ **c.57** The Christian apostle and missionary Paul, a Roman citizen, is sent for trial to Rome and eventually executed under Emperor Nero.

✕ **61** The Iceni tribe in Britain revolt under their leader Boudicca (Boadicea).

✳ **79** The volcano Vesuvius erupts, burying the Roman towns of Pompeii and Herculaneum on Italy's west coast.

✳ **c.60** The inventor Hero of Alexandria designs a steam engine.

✳ **c.80–95** Wheat, olive, and grape production is boosted across Roman Africa, making the region the granary of Rome.

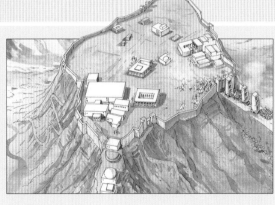

✕ **70** Jerusalem is captured by imperial troops following a Jewish revolt against Roman rule. The last rebels commit suicide rather than surrender at Masada (–73).

👑 **97** A Chinese diplomatic mission sets out for Roman Syria but gets only as far as Characene, a state at the head of the Persian Gulf.

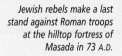

Jewish rebels make a last stand against Roman troops at the hilltop fortress of Masada in 73 A.D.

👑 **c.78** Kanishka becomes ruler of the Kushans. He boosts the wealth of the empire by diverting silk caravans from China through his territories.

📖 **c.90** Greek-influenced art, including statues of the Buddha, is created at Gandhara, a region in what is now northwestern Pakistan.

👑 **57** Chinese chronicles record a visit to the imperial court by Japanese emissaries.

✳ **c.70** Work begins on China's Grand Canal, which eventually reaches a length of more than 1,100 miles (1,800 km).

✳ **c.80** The Chinese make primitive compasses from lodestone, a magnetic iron ore. They were probably used in divination rather than for navigation.

✳ **c.100** The Chinese make an insecticide from dried chrysanthemum flowers; its active ingredient, pyrethrum, is still widely used as an insecticide that is virtually harmless to birds and mammals.

AMERICAS

EUROPE

AFRICA

WESTERN ASIA

SOUTH & CENTRAL ASIA

EAST ASIA & OCEANIA

0–100 A.D.   27

THE ROMAN EMPIRE

U NDER THE RULE OF THE EMPERORS *Rome set about expanding its power. By the beginning of the 2nd century* A.D. *its empire stretched from the north of England to southern Egypt and from Spain to Syria; never before had so many different peoples lived together under one government. In their heyday Rome's emperors presided over an era of relative peace and prosperity in which national differences gradually weakened as Roman citizenship was progressively extended to all the empire's provinces.*

▲ A grandnephew of Julius Caesar, Octavian rose to power in the civil war that followed Caesar's assassination in 44 B.C. By 31 B.C. he had defeated all his rivals and was ruling Rome in effect as a dictator. Taking the title Augustus ("revered one"), he was to be the first Roman emperor, bringing to an end almost 500 years of republican rule.

When Augustus became Rome's first emperor, he made a pretence of restoring republican government while continuing to hold all real power himself. He was supreme commander of the army, which included a new personal bodyguard, the Praetorian Guard.

Augustus stamped out corruption, established a civil service, and rebuilt Rome. But his death exposed the weakness of a system that depended on the emperor's personal qualities for its success. Over the next 50 years Rome's rulers included Caligula, who made his favorite horse a consul, and Nero, who murdered his mother and two of his wives.

Despite the flaws of some of its rulers, the empire continued to grow. One reason lay in the efficiency of the administrative machine Augustus had created. The empire's main prop, however, was the Roman army, which was by far the most efficient fighting machine of its day; its disciplined legions, staffed by highly trained career soldiers, rarely failed to defeat their less organized opponents. Britain was conquered by legionaries in 43 A.D., Dacia (Romania) in 106,

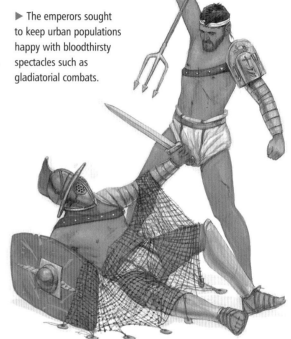

► The emperors sought to keep urban populations happy with bloodthirsty spectacles such as gladiatorial combats.

👑 **27 B.C.** Having defeated his rival Mark Antony, Octavian takes the title of Augustus and is granted additional powers. The imperial period of Roman history is often dated from this year.

📖 **19** The poet Virgil completes the *Aeneid*, the greatest Roman epic.

⚔ **19** The Roman general Agrippa completes the conquest of Spain.

⚔ **9 A.D.** The German leader Hermann (Arminius in Latin) destroys three legions at the Battle of the Teutoburg Forest, the worst defeat suffered by Rome's army in early imperial times.

Roman Roads

"They have built paved roads throughout the country," the Greek geographer Strabo reported in the 1st century A.D., "leveling ridges and filling up hollows so as to make possible the movement of heavily loaded wagons." Road building was indeed one of the Romans' supreme achievements, providing highways that allowed their legions to cover over 30 miles (50 km) on foot a day. Roadbeds were layered (*inset, right*), with the paving stones resting on beds of sand and gravel; the surface was cambered to allow rainwater to run off into gutters.

Armenia and Parthia (northwest Persia) by 117. In the wake of military victory taxes and tributes poured into Rome. The emperors spent some of this wealth on massive building projects. They also used their wealth to buy public support, handing out free grain and paying for lavish gladiatorial games.

If Rome grew rich from its conquests, many of its provinces also prospered under early imperial rule. In return for paying taxes, their citizens received the protection of the world's mightiest military power. In regions where city living had long been established, merchants found a huge new export market for their goods. In more remote areas the Romans introduced the benefits of urban living. Most large provincial towns had Roman-style public buildings, including amphitheaters, law courts, and public baths.

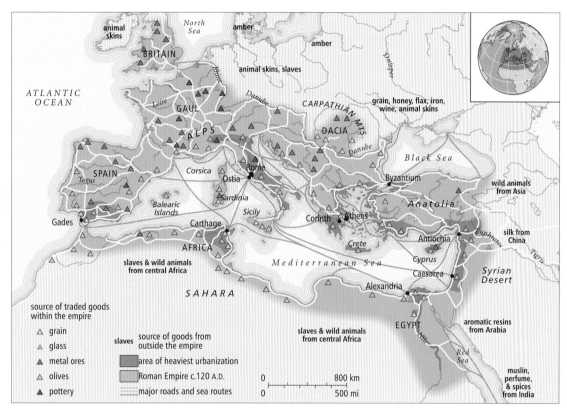

◄ In an age of horse and sail power the Roman Empire was a triumph of good communications as much as of military might. Covering more than 3 million square miles (5 million sq. km) at its peak, its network of paved roads and well-used sea routes provided not just highways for the legions but also vital arteries for trade.

👑 **14** Augustus dies and is succeeded as emperor by the 55-year-old Tiberius.

👑 **37** Tiberius is succeeded by the crazed Caligula, who, two years later, proclaims himself a god.

👑 **41** Caligula is murdered by soldiers of the Praetorian Guard (his own bodyguard), who replace him with his uncle, Claudius.

✕ **43** A Roman army under the emperor Claudius conquers Britain.

👑 **54** Claudius dies, reputedly poisoned by his own wife, to be replaced by Nero, her 17-year-old son by a previous husband.

☀ **64** Much of Rome is destroyed by a fire. The emperor Nero blames the disaster on Christians.

👑 **68** Nero is deposed by an army revolt. The Year of the Four Emperors follows, a time of anarchy ended when Vespasian seizes power.

✳ **80** The Colosseum, an amphitheater holding over 50,000 spectators, is completed in Rome.

✕ **106** The Emperor Trajan conquers Dacia (Romania).

✕ **117** The conquests of Armenia and Parthia (northwest Persia) mark the high point of imperial expansion.

👑 **117** On the death of Trajan the new emperor, Hadrian, abandons the policy of further expanding the empire.

👑 **122** In Britain work begins on Hadrian's Wall, built to protect Roman England from unconquered tribes to the north.

👑 **138** Antoninus comes to the imperial throne. His 23-year reign is a time of peace and prosperity.

👑 **161** The philosopher-emperor Marcus Aurelius succeeds Antoninus and continues his humanitarian policies.

👑 **212** All free adult males in the empire are granted Roman citizenship.

AMERICAS

⊛ **c.120** The Moche people of northern Peru now control vast areas of lowland; they produce gold and silver artifacts, pottery, and textiles.

☀ **c.150** At Teotihuacán in Mexico, work gets under way on the Pyramid of the Sun; it will become the largest building in pre-Columbian America.

EUROPE

📖 **c.100** The Roman historian Tacitus begins his *Histories*, chronicling the history of the empire from 68 to 96 A.D.

⚔ **c.101** The Roman Emperor Trajan begins his campaign against the Kingdom of Dacia, north of the Danube River, which becomes a Roman province in 106.

📖 **113** In Rome Trajan's Column is built; the spiraling reliefs carved around it depict the story of Trajan's wars against Dacia.

Under a succession of talented rulers—Trajan, Hadrian, Antoninus, and Marcus Aurelius—the Roman Empire enjoyed its heyday in the 2nd century. Its greatness was founded on trade as much as on military success. This marble carving of a merchant ship comes from Trajan's Column in Rome.

⚔ **115** The Jews of Cyprus, Egypt, Cyrene (Libya), and Mesopotamia revolt against the rule of Trajan and the Romans (– 117).

👑 **117** Hadrian becomes Roman emperor, ruling to 138; he builds stone and turf walls to protect his borders in Germany and Britain.

📖 **c.120** Plutarch, the Greek historian, biographer, and philosopher, dies; his famed *Parallel Lives* describes and compares 46 great figures from Greek and Roman history.

AFRICA

⊛ **c.100** By this date Greco-Roman merchants are sailing to East Africa for ivory.

⊛ **168** Claudius Ptolemy, Egyptian astronomer and geographer, dies. His legacy is the Earth-centered view of the universe that becomes known as the Ptolemaic System.

⚔ **173** In Egypt shepherd brigands stage revolts against the Roman Empire; they are crushed by governor Avidius Cassius.

WESTERN ASIA

👑 **106** The Kingdom of Nabataea, whose capital is Petra, is annexed by the Romans to become the province of Arabia.

⚔ **115** In this year and the next the Roman Emperor Trajan wages a dramatically successful military campaign against the Parthians, capturing their capital of Ctesiphon and putting a puppet ruler on the throne.

⚔ **134** In Cappadocia (eastern Turkey) Roman troops repel an attack by Alans from southeast Russia.

⚔ **193** The governor of Syria, Pescennius Niger, is declared emperor by part of the Roman army, but is defeated and executed soon afterward.

SOUTH & CENTRAL ASIA

Reliquary dating from Kanishka's reign, c.100 A.D.

👑 **c. 100** Under Kanishka the Kushan Empire reaches its greatest extent, stretching from the Aral Sea to the Ganges River. The king promotes the spread of Mahayana Buddhism through Central Asia.

👑 **107** The Roman Emperor Trajan sends envoys to India (presumably to Kanishka).

EAST ASIA & OCEANIA

☀ **c.100** Buddhism begins to spread in China.

⊛ **109** The earliest extant example of Chinese hemp paper with writing on it dates from this year.

👑 **120** China is by this time the largest and most densely populated state in the world.

☀ **c.148** An Qing (Anshigao), a Parthian missionary and translator, actively seeks converts to Buddhism at the Chinese court and in the area around the capital, Luoyang.

👑 **c.150** The city of El Mirador is abandoned; Tikal replaces it as the chief Mayan center in Central America's Petén lowlands.

👑 **c.200** The eruption of Mt. Ilopango precipitates the decline of the southern Maya of modern-day Guatemala.

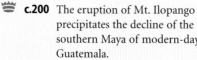

⊕ **133** Hadrian's Wall across northern Britain is completed.

📖 **c.140** Death of Juvenal, the Roman lawyer and satirical writer; his *Satires* rail against Roman vices and society's evils.

📖 **c.190** One of the earliest examples of Christian figurative art, a fresco on the arch in the Catacomb of Santa Priscilla in Rome, is completed. Four men and three women are seated around a table; the central figure is breaking bread.

⚔ **192** The despotic Emperor Commodus is strangled by the Roman athlete Narcissus, bring the Antonine Dynasty to an end.

👑 **197** The governor of Britain, Clodius Albinus, declared emperor by his troops, vies for power with Septimius Severus. By defeating him, Severus reunites the Roman Empire.

The Roman Emperor Hadrian, shown in profile on a coin.

⊕ **c.190** Ironworking in Africa spreads as far south as the Limpopo Valley in southern Africa.

👑 **c.200** The Kingdom of Axum in Ethiopia is now a major power in the area, trading with the Roman Empire, Arabia, and India through its Red Sea port, Adulis.

⚔ **197** The Parthian capital Ctesiphon (in modern-day Iraq) is sacked by Septimius Severus, who was proclaimed Roman emperor in 193.

👑 **198** Northern Mesopotamia becomes a Roman province.

Septimius Severus, conqueror of the Parthians.

⚔ **c.130** The Saka state in western India wins control of Ujain in central India.

📖 **c.150** Date of the earliest known Sanskrit inscription, carved on the orders of the Saka King Rudraman at Junagadh in western India.

⊕ **c.200** On the Deccan Plateau in India cities appear for the first time.

⚔ **184** Peasant farmers known as the Yellow Turbans rebel, challenging the corruption and ineffectual leadership of the Han court. The revolt is suppressed, but the Han Dynasty is greatly weakened.

⚔ **189** General Dong Zhuo seizes power in the Han capital, Luoyang, presiding over a vicious dictatorship fronted by a puppet ruler, 15-year-old Emperor Xian.

👑 **c.200** The Kingdom of Champa is founded in what is now central Vietnam. It will becomes the most enduring Hinduized state in Southeast Asia.

AMERICAS

EUROPE

AFRICA

WESTERN ASIA

SOUTH & CENTRAL ASIA

EAST ASIA & OCEANIA

100–200 A.D.

THE JEWISH DIASPORA

S OME HISTORIANS DATE THE START *of the Diaspora, or "dispersal," of the Jewish people as far back as 586 B.C., when many Jews were forced into exile in Babylon in the "Babylonian captivity." The next millennium witnessed several other forcible dispersals, particularly after unsuccessful uprisings against Roman rule in Judea in 66–73 A.D. and 132–135 A.D. In addition, many Jews chose to leave their homeland voluntarily in order to live and work in wealthier countries. By 500 A.D. Jewish communities were established in lands from southern Spain to the borders of India.*

▲ One of the treasures seized by Jerusalem's Roman conquerors in 70 A.D. was the seven-branched golden lampstand, or menorah, that had graced the city's Temple. In future centuries the menorah would become an enduring symbol of Jewish cultural identity.

▶ The Diaspora saw Jews moving out from Israel to locations around the Mediterranean world and also deep into Asia. The area around Babylon in the ancient Mesopotamian lands became an important Jewish center; so did Alexandria in Egypt.

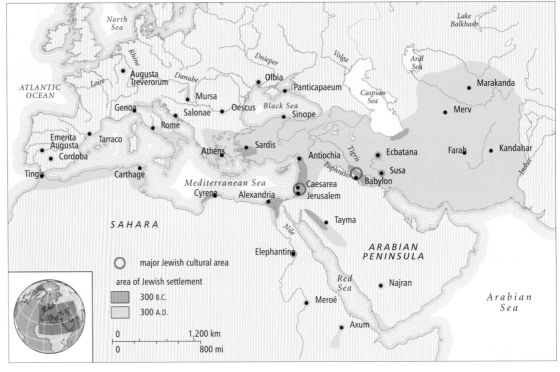

major Jewish cultural area

area of Jewish settlement
- 300 B.C.
- 300 A.D.

| 0 | 1,200 km |
| 0 | 800 mi |

🜲 **332 B.C.** Alexander the Great conquers the Bible lands in the course of defeating the Persian Empire. In the ensuing Hellenistic (Greek) Period, Jewish people are encouraged to embrace Greek culture.

🜲 **323** On Alexander's death the Bible lands fall under the control of the Ptolemies—Greek rulers of Egypt.

🜲 **198** The Seleucids—Greek rulers of western Asia—wrest control of the Bible lands from the Ptolemies.

🜲 **175** Antiochos IV becomes Seleucid emperor; in the course of his 12-year reign he proscribes the Jewish religion, attempting to force worship of the Greek gods on the Jews.

✕ **167** Judas Maccabeus leads a Jewish uprising (the Maccabean Revolt) against Antiochos's measures.

✕ **164** The Maccabean rebels win back and rededicate the Temple in Jerusalem, which had temporarily been given over to the Greek god Zeus.

🜲 **142** Judas Maccabeus's brother Simon establishes an independent Jewish state under the rule of the Hasmonean Dynasty.

✕ **63** The Roman general Pompey forces the Hasmoneans to accept Rome's authority over the lands the Romans call Judea.

🜲 **40** The Roman Senate appoints Herod as king of Judea, replacing the last king of the Hasmonean line.

🜲 **4** Herod dies, and his kingdom is divided among three of his sons.

In the centuries following the Babylonian Captivity Judah and Israel fell under the control of a series of foreign powers. First they formed part of the Persian Empire; when that succumbed to Alexander the Great, they came under Greek control. In the 2nd century B.C. Maccabean rebels, taking their name from their leader Judas Maccabeus, were able to establish a semi-independent state; but in 63 B.C. the Hasmonean Dynasty that ruled it was forced to accept the overlordship of a fresh imperial master, and the Bible lands became the Roman province of Judea.

Since their own homeland was too small to hold a large population, many Jews were drawn to cities such as Egypt's Alexandria, founded by Alexander the Great in 331 B.C., in search of a better life. The communities of the Diaspora centered on the synagogue (meeting house) and courts of law; Jewish people often lived in a separate quarter of their adopted city. In general they were free to follow their laws and religious practices, although in the Hellenistic Period (323–30 B.C.) Jews were encouraged to adopt a Greek lifestyle.

The Roman era in Jewish history began with Jerusalem's fall to the Roman general Pompey in 63 B.C. In 66 A.D. its inhabitants launched a revolt against Roman rule that was savagely suppressed; Vespasian and his son Titus, both future Roman emperors, led the Roman forces, which captured Jerusalem after a 139-day siege and largely destroyed it, deporting Jews to Syria and Italy.

A further uprising in 132 A.D., this one led by Simeon bar Kokba, was also put down bloodily. In its wake Judea was renamed Palestine, and Jerusalem became a Roman city that Jews were forbidden to enter. Thereafter more than 1,800 years would pass before an independent Jewish state would be reestablished in the region.

The Dead Sea Scrolls

In 1947 a shepherd made a remarkable discovery near Qumran, 10 miles (16 km) south of Jericho in the Dead Sea region. In caves on a cliff face he found clay jars containing ancient parchment scrolls; over the next 10 years others would be discovered in caverns nearby. The texts—mainly written on parchment, some on papyrus—were dated by experts mostly to about 100 B.C. They included copies of the Hebrew Bible and writings describing the beliefs of a Jewish sect that had lived at Qumran from about 130 B.C. to 70 A.D. This sect—the Essenes—believed that they had been chosen by God to survive the "end of days." The scrolls probably formed their library, stored for safekeeping at a time when war with Rome was raging nearby.

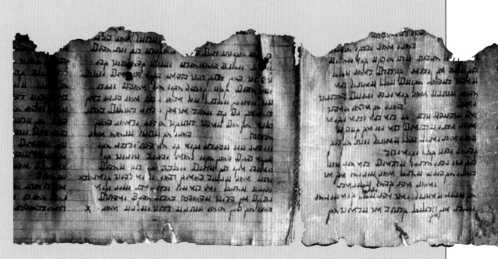

👑 **44 A.D.** Rome assumes direct rule over all of Judea.

⚔ **66** The First Jewish Revolt breaks out against Roman rule.

⚔ **70** Jerusalem falls to Roman forces under the future Emperor Titus after a 139-day siege. The Temple is destroyed, and many Jews are forced into exile.

⚔ **73** The last of the Jewish rebels commit mass suicide at the clifftop fortress of Masada in southern Judea to avoid having to surrender to Roman troops.

⚔ **115–117** Diaspora Jews in North Africa, Cyprus, and Mesopotamia rise up unsuccessfully against the rule of the Emperor Trajan.

⚔ **132** In Judea the Second Jewish Revolt breaks out under the leadership of Simeon bar Kokba, seen as a messiah or Jewish national savior.

⚔ **135** The bar Kokba revolt is crushed by Roman forces. In its wake Judea is renamed Palestine, and its former Jewish population is scattered; Jews are forbidden to enter Jerusalem.

☀ **c.200** The Mishnah, a collection of Jewish oral law that makes up part of the Talmud, is compiled.

☀ **219** Babylonia becomes the focus of Jewish life with the establishment of the first Jewish academy at Sura.

☀ **388** The Romans pass legislation forbidding intermarriage between Christians and Jews.

☀ **476** As the Roman Empire collapses, the definitive edition of the Talmud—the most authoritative compilation of Jewish oral law—is compiled in Babylon.

AMERICAS

Noted for its lively artworks, including this vase scene of a religious ritual, the Moche Culture takes its name from a Peruvian river valley. At its peak in the 3rd century its influence stretched over much of northern Peru.

c.200 The Moche state in northern Peru moves into its most influential era; the culture is notable for its gigantic mud-brick (adobe) ceremonial platforms.

EUROPE

205 Plotinus, the Neoplatonist philosopher, is born. He will study in Alexandria before settling in Rome in 244, becoming a popular teacher and producing a collection of philosophical essays, the *Enneads*.

212 Roman citizenship is extended to everyone living within the empire's boundaries in an attempt to raise more taxes.

260 The Roman Emperor Valerian, marching against the Persians, is defeated at Edessa (eastern Turkey).

267 The Goths, a Germanic tribe occupying the Black Sea region (the Ukraine and modern Bulgaria), make one of several incursions into Roman territory, pillaging Thrace, Macedonia, and Greece.

AFRICA

203 During a persecution of Christians ordered by the Emperor Septimius Severus, Perpetua and her pregnant slave Felicitas are martyred at Carthage.

248 Anti-Christian rioting breaks out in Alexandria.

250 The Emperor Decius issues an edict against Christians, forcing Cyprian, bishop of Carthage, into hiding. In the course of a further persecution in 258 Cyprian is executed.

WESTERN ASIA

c.200 The Mishnah, a collection of Jewish oral law that forms part of the Talmud, takes its final form.

219 The first Jewish academy is established at Sura; Babylonia becomes the focus of Jewish spiritual life.

224 The Parthian realm is overthrown by Ardashir I, from Fars in Persia, who founds the Sassanian Empire.

226 Ctesiphon, previously the winter capital of the Parthian emperors, becomes the Sassanian capital until 637.

240 Shapur I, son of Ardashir I, becomes Sassanian emperor.

c.250 A series of wall paintings illustrating biblical narratives is created to decorate the interior of the synagogue at Dura-Europos.

c.260 The capture of Emperor Valerian by the Sassanians at Edessa is commemorated in a cliff-face carving at the Persian site now known as Naqsh-i Rustam.

269 Zenobia, queen of Palmyra, conquers Egypt; the following year she conquers many of Rome's eastern provinces in Asia Minor, enthroning her son as eastern emperor.

SOUTH & CENTRAL ASIA

c.200 Over the next century Hindu laws are systematized.

c.213 Vasudeva, last of the great Kushan emperors, dies; the Kushan Empire is divided into western and eastern parts.

c.224 Kushan territories in Bactria and northern India are seized by the Sassanian Shapur I (to 240).

EAST ASIA & OCEANIA

220 The last Han emperor is deposed and the empire divided into three separate kingdoms.

239 Himiko, queen of a Japanese state known from Chinese sources as "Yamatai," sends a friendly mission to China.

259 Buddhists from China begin to make pilgrimages to India.

Earthenware model of an ox cart, Jin Dynasty, China.

👑 **c.250** By this time Teotihuacán has developed into a major urban center laid out on a grid pattern, with residential blocks surrounding a central avenue of palaces and temples.

⊛ **c.300** Commemorative steles—stone pillars—are erected in the central lowland forest area by the Maya; the earliest found is at Tikal.

⊛ **c.300** For the first time Mayan builders incorporate corbeled arches and vaults in their constructions.

AMERICAS

👑 **286** Troubled by barbarian attacks, the Emperor Diocletian divides the Roman Empire into western and eastern parts, appointing Maximian to rule the west.

👑 **287** Marcus Aurelius Carausius, commander of the Roman fleet in the English Channel, stages an unsuccessful rebellion, finally put down by Diocletian in 296.

The Roman Empire's corulers, Diocletian and Maximian.

EUROPE

👑 **c.250** Aphilas becomes king of Axum and conquers surrounding territories. The kingdom begins to mint its own coins in gold and silver.

⚔ **260** Pirate raids are launched on North Africa by Franks who have seized ships at Tarraco (Tarragona in modern Spain).

☀ **c.270** St. Anthony becomes a hermit in the Egyptian desert; in the years to come, many others will follow him into the wilderness.

AFRICA

For over 400 years, from its foundation in 224 A.D., Persia's Sassanian Empire rivaled Rome for influence in western Asia. Taking their name from Sassan, the dynasty's founder, its rulers—one of whom is shown (*right*) hunting rams—embraced the Zoroastrian religion and sought to revive the glories of the Persian Empire created by Cyrus the Great seven centuries earlier. To the east the empire confronted the threat of the Central Asian nomads; one such people, the Ephthalite Huns, briefly forced its rulers into subjection in the late 5th century.

⚔ **272** Zenobia, having been defeated in several battles and besieged at Palmyra, is captured by the Roman Emperor Aurelian. A lively and beautiful woman, she is feted by the Romans and lives out her days in comfort in Italy.

WESTERN ASIA

⚔ **c.225** The empire of the Satakani or Andhra Dynasty, which has ruled substantial territories in the Deccan and southern India for almost 300 years, breaks up.

👑 **c.270** The Kushans lose control of the plains around the Ganges River.

SOUTH & CENTRAL ASIA

⚔ **263** Wei, straddling the Yellow River Valley, is the strongest of China's three kingdoms, conquering the weaker Shu Kingdom to the south.

👑 **265** In China the Wei general Sima Yan is enthroned as Wudi, the first emperor of the Jin Dynasty.

⚔ **280** Wu, the third of the Chinese kingdoms created in 220, is conquered by the Jin, thus reunifying China under the victorious general Sima Yan.

⚔ **291** After Sima Yan's death his sons battle for control, enlisting support from the steppe peoples beyond China's boundaries; the northern kingdom breaks up into Chinese and nomad states.

👑 **c.300** Easter Island is settled.

EAST ASIA & OCEANIA

200–300 A.D.

THE INDIAN EMPIRES

▲ This capital once topped a 50-foot (15-m) high pillar set up by the emperor Ashoka at Sarnath in the Ganges Valley, where the Buddha first preached. Ashoka had several dozen such pillars erected around his realm.

IN 500 B.C. THE INDIAN SUBCONTINENT *was a land of petty kingdoms, the wealthiest of which were concentrated in the Ganges and Indus river valleys. In the course of the next millennium two great empires—those of the Mauryas and of the Guptas—would for a time impose some unity on the divided states. The Mauryan rulers helped spread the Buddhist faith, but the later Guptas encouraged a revival of Hinduism.*

Hinduism had originated in the 2nd millennium B.C. with the Aryans, a pastoral people who produced the first Hindu scriptures. These works—the Vedas—laid down a "caste" system of hereditary social ranks, with the priestly class of Brahmins at the top and a fixed hierarchy of warriors, merchants, and servants beneath them. By 500 B.C. people irked by the rigidities of the caste system had begun to resent the power wielded by those at the top; they turned to less hierarchical new sects, such as Buddhism and Jainism.

At this time some 16 states dominated northern India, of which Magadha, straddling the Ganges Valley, was the most strategically and economically important. In about 321 B.C. Chandragupta Maurya seized the throne there. His efficiently run empire was administered by a civil service; it had a huge army that in time came to include up to 600,000 infantrymen and 9,000 elephants. Chandragupta ruled from a vast royal city surrounded by a moat and a timber palisade. By the time he passed on the throne to his son in about 300, his empire stretched

over much of the continent, including some of the lands on India's northwestern frontier that had been captured by Alexander the Great just 35 years before.

Chandragupta's grandson Ashoka, who reigned from about 269 to 232 B.C., was another great Mauryan ruler. His kingdom extended over most of the subcontinent. He conquered Kalinga in eastern India, but was so shocked by the suffering caused by the fighting that he decided to convert to Buddhism, which preached nonviolence. Ashoka set up stone pillars along pilgrimage routes; they carried carved messages urging compassion, respect for all animal life, considerate behavior, and courtesy to all.

By 185 B.C. the Mauryan Empire had collapsed, and the region dissolved into small kingdoms under a series of weaker dynasties. It was not until the 4th century A.D. that the next great empire arose, when a marriage alliance brought another ruler named Chandragupta—no relation to the Mauryan emperor of that name—control of Magadha. By the time of Chandragupta II, who reigned from 380 to 414

---

c.321 B.C. From a power base in northwestern India Chandragupta Maurya seizes control of the kingdom of Magadha and founds the Mauryan Empire.

c.305 Chandragupta signs a peace treaty with Alexander the Great's successor Seleucus; by its terms the Mauryans receive much of today's Afghanistan and Pakistan in return for their alliance and a corps of 500 war elephants.

c.300 Chandragupta hands the throne to his son Bindusara, who further extends Mauryan rule into India's deep south.

c.269 Bindusara's son Ashoka ascends the throne.

c.261 Ashoka conquers Kalinga, a previously independent kingdom on India's east coast, in a battle said to have cost the lives of 100,000 men.

c.259 Sickened by the violence of his victory, Ashoka converts to Buddhism.

c.250 Ashoka sends Buddhist missionaries to Ceylon (Sri Lanka).

c.232 Ashoka's death marks the start of the Mauryan Empire's decline.

c.185 The decline of the Mauryan Empire culminates in the overthrow of the last Mauryan ruler; the region dissolves into smaller kingdoms.

c.183 The Greek rulers of Bactria, a breakaway province of the Seleucid Kingdom, briefly reconquer the lands ceded to the Mauryans by Seleucus a century before.

c.135 The Sakas, a nomadic people from Central Asia, conquer Bactria from the Greeks.

c.100 By this time the Sakas have established a powerful kingdom in northern India.

50 A.D. At about this date the Kushans, nomads originally from China, invade northwestern India, defeating the northernmost Sakas and establishing an empire of their own.

A Buddhist Holy Site

In 1818 the first of a large group of Buddhist monuments was uncovered at Sanchi in central India. The remarkably well preserved buildings offered a fascinating record of the development of Buddhist art and architecture over some 1,300 years. The Mauryan Emperor Ashoka was probably the first to build on the site. He erected an inscribed pillar and a stupa—a solid dome of masonry built to encase relics of the Buddha or other Buddhist holy men. In the 2nd century B.C. a stone railing was built around the stupa, along with four elaborately carved gateways depicting scenes from the Buddha's life; a second stupa was also built at this time. Pilgrims walked clockwise around the stupas as an act of veneration.

A.D., the Gupta realm rivaled the Mauryan Empire in its extent. The Guptas were strong patrons of the arts and sciences, and they were also devout Hindus. The period became known as a golden age in India for literature, architecture, astronomy, and mathematics, heralding what has been called a "Hindu renaissance."

▶ Gupta rule expanded from the Ganges Valley across much of northern and eastern India in the 4th century A.D.

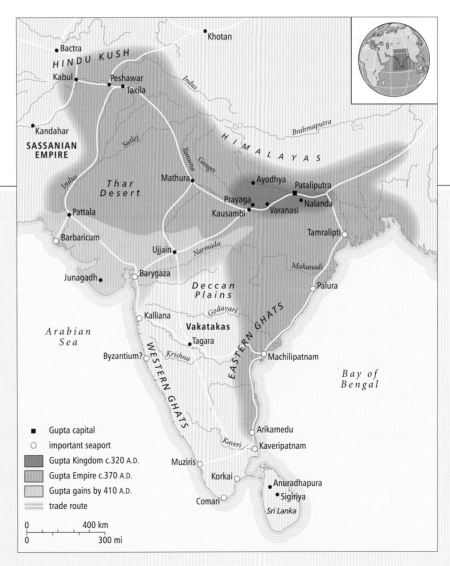

☀ **c.100** The Kushan Empire reaches its peak under the Buddhist Kanishka, who promotes the spread of Buddhism throughout Central Asia.

👑 **320** Chandragupta I, the founder of the Gupta Empire, expands his kingdom from a small heartland on the southern banks of the Ganges River (–335).

👑 **335** In the course of a 45-year reign Chandragupta's son Samudragupta conquers much of northern and eastern India, bringing the Kushan Empire to an end (–380).

👑 **380** The Gupta Empire reaches a peak under Chandragupta II, almost rivaling the Mauryan Empire in size (–414).

⚔ **510** The Ephthalite Huns invade the Gupta lands, bringing the empire to an end.

300–400 A.D.

AMERICAS

 c.300 Latest date proposed for the Hohokam Culture's emergence in the American Southwest. Its ball courts and temple mounds show a Mexican influence.

 c.300 The city of Teotihuacán is by now the most powerful state in central Mexico.

c.300 In the highlands of South America around what is now the Peru–Bolivia border a new urban center is emerging at Tiahuanaco, on the southern shores of Lake Titicaca.

EUROPE

The Emperor Constantine celebrated victory over Maxentius, his rival for imperial power, at the Milvian Bridge in 312 A.D. by ordering the construction of this monumental arch in Rome. The battle also greatly helped the cause of Christianity, since Constantine had reportedly seen a vision of the cross before the fighting started. In the following year he issued the Edict of Milan, confirming religious toleration throughout the Western Roman Empire.

305 The Roman Emperor Diocletian abdicates.

306 The army in Britain proclaims Constantine as Augustus (co-emperor) in the west following the death of his father Constantius.

313 Constantine issues the Edict of Milan granting toleration to Christians in the Western Empire.

324 Constantine becomes sole emperor following the defeat and execution of Licinius, emperor in the east.

AFRICA

305 Donatus, bishop of Casa Negra, teaches that only those without sin belong in the church; his Donatist doctrines will split Africa's Christian community for much of the century.

c.350 The Kingdom of Meroë in Nubia (present-day Sudan) collapses after being conquered by Axum; Nubia splits into three states: Nobatia, Makkura, and Alwa.

c.350 King Ezana of Axum is baptized a Christian; converted by missionary monks from Syria, he is the earliest known Christian in sub-Saharan Africa.

WESTERN ASIA

c.303 The Kingdom of Armenia becomes the first country to adopt Christianity as an official religion.

348 Shapur II, Sassanian ruler of Persia, defeats the Emperor Constantius at Singara, but fails to drive the Romans from Mesopotamia.

c.350 White (Ephthalite) Huns begin raiding across the eastern Persian border.

SOUTH & CENTRAL ASIA

320 In the vacuum left by the collapse of Kushan power Chandragupta I, founder of India's Gupta Dynasty, creates a powerful Hindu kingdom on the Ganges Plain (– 335).

335 The Gupta King Samudragupta, reigning to 380, fights major campaigns in northern and eastern India.

EAST ASIA & OCEANIA

 c.300 In Japan the Yamato kings extend their power throughout the island of Honshu; they build large "keyhole" tombs.

 c.300 The stirrup is introduced to China by horse-riding nomads.

Bronze statue of a horseman from Gansu, western China.

c.300 Over the following century northern China fragments into a mosaic of warring states.

313 In Korea the former Han colony of Luolong falls to the powerful northern Korean state of Koguryo.

👑 **c.400** In the eastern woodlands of North America the Hopewell mound-building culture passes its prime as the trade network sustaining it starts to break down.

AMERICAS

👑 **330** Constantine founds the city of Constantinople on the Bosporus strait between Europe and Asia.

☀ **361** The Emperor Julian attempts to revive paganism in the Roman Empire (– 363).

✗ **c.372** The Huns, nomadic horsemen from Central Asia, conquer the Ostrogoths of the Black Sea area.

☀ **391** The Emperor Theodosius I officially ends paganism within the Roman Empire.

👑 **395** On the death of Theodosius the empire is permanently divided into eastern and western halves.

👑 **395** Stilicho, a successful Roman general of barbarian origin, becomes virtual ruler of the Western Empire as guardian to Honorius, Theodosius's son, emperor in the west.

✗ **396** The Visigoths, led by Alaric, rampage through the Balkans and Greece (– 398).

Half Vandal by birth, Stilicho was the Western Empire's true ruler in the late 4th century.

EUROPE

Axum was a major African power in the 4th and 5th centuries, dominating the Red Sea trade routes. After its ruler Ezana converted to Christianity, the kingdom became a bastion of the faith famed for its rock-cut churches (*right*). As such, it held out against the Islamic conquests of the 7th century, eventually forming the basis of the Christian Kingdom of Ethiopia.

☀ **391** Christianity is proclaimed the official religion of Egypt. Many temples of the old gods are destroyed.

✳ **c.400** Iron is produced at Castle Cavern, a site in present-day South Africa.

AFRICA

✗ **363** Constantius's successor, Julian, invades Persia; he is killed in battle, and Shapur II regains control of eastern Mesopotamia.

✗ **c.370** The Huns move westward from the borders of China, encroaching on the Ostrogoths inhabiting the Russian steppes.

WESTERN ASIA

☀ **c.350** Dunhuang, an oasis town at the edge of the Gobi Desert on the Silk Road from China to the Mediterranean, becomes a flourishing Buddhist center.

✗ **380** Chandragupta II succeeds Samudragupta. During his 34-year reign he will conquer the Sakas of western India, bringing the Gupta Empire to its peak.

☀ **c.400** Hinduism revives in India under Gupta patronage; there is a flowering of classical Sanskrit literature.

SOUTH & CENTRAL ASIA

👑 **c.350** Funan (in present-day Cambodia and southern Vietnam) is the most powerful state in Southeast Asia.

✗ **369** According to a later Japanese source, a Yamato army invades southern Korea.

☀ **372** Buddhism reaches the Korean Peninsula.

✗ **386** Toba nomads invade northern China (– 397) and establish a state in Wei on the northern frontier.

☀ **399** A Chinese Buddhist monk, Fa-hsien, travels by foot along the Silk Road from China to India and back (– 413).

EAST ASIA & OCEANIA

300–400 A.D.

THE SPREAD OF CHRISTIANITY

CHRISTIANITY IS THE RELIGION *based on the teachings of Jesus Christ, a charismatic figure who preached and healed the sick in the towns and villages of Palestine, then part of the Roman Empire, in the first third of the 1st century A.D. His religious and political views were unacceptable to many of his fellow Jews, as well as to the Romans, and in about 30 A.D. he was condemned to death and crucified.*

▲ In this 2nd-century carving the familiar Christian sign of the cross is combined with the *chi-rho* symbol (displayed within the ring), which combines the Greek letters making up the initial characters of Christ's name.

Jesus's followers, the Christians, believed that he was the Messiah, or son of God, who had risen from the dead. They began meeting in small groups to spread his teachings and the news of his resurrection. In the first decades after his death the new religion began to spread outside Palestine. Its first great missionary was Paul of Tarsus, a Roman citizen from a well-to-do Jewish family. Paul traveled throughout the eastern Mediterranean as far as Rome itself to preach the Christian gospel to Jews and non-Jews alike.

The Roman authorities distrusted the early Christians because they refused to submit to the official state religion and to make sacrifices to the Roman gods. In 64 A.D. the Emperor Nero blamed them for starting a fire that destroyed much of the city of Rome, and many Christians were rounded up and executed. It was the first of a series of mass persecutions of Christians carried out by the Roman authorities over the next 250 years. As a result, the early Christians lived and worshiped in secret, adopting clandestine emblems such as the sign of a fish to identify their places of worship to each other. These signs can still be seen carved on the walls of the catacombs, their underground cemeteries, in Rome.

The last great persecution of Christians took place under the Emperor Diocletian in 303. Shortly afterward the Emperor Constantine adopted a policy of toleration throughout the empire. From then on Christianity could be practiced openly, and the faith witnessed a period of rapid growth.

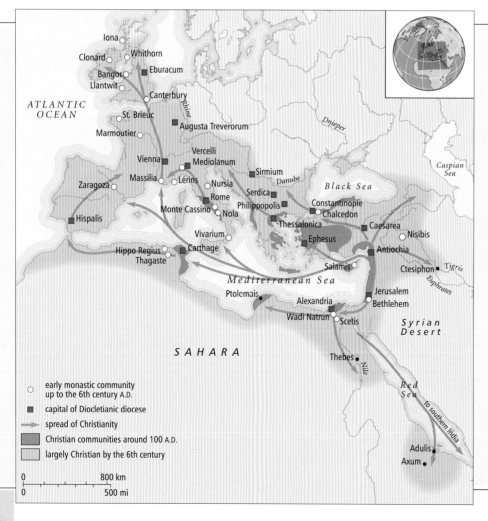

c.30 A.D. Jesus is crucified in Jerusalem; Peter, his disciple, brings his followers together in the days after his death.

c.46–62 Paul makes four missionary journeys, founding churches in Syria, Asia Minor, Macedonia, and Greece, and visiting Rome.

c.49 Jesus's followers hold a council in Jerusalem in which it is decided not to impose Jewish law on non-Jewish Christians.

c.60–100 The four Gospels, telling the story of Jesus's life and death, are written down at this time.

64 Nero executes Christians after a great fire in Rome; Peter, the first bishop of Rome, is believed to have died in this persecution.

◄ Christiantity spread from its original base on the Mediterranean's eastern shores across the Roman Empire and also into Armenia and Axum (Ethiopia).

Map labels

Iona, Clonard, Whithorn, Bangor, Eburacum, Llantwit, Canterbury, St. Brieuc, Marmoutier, Augusta Treverorum, Vercelli, Vienna, Mediolanum, Sirmium, Massilia, Lérins, Nursia, Zaragoza, Rome, Serdica, Monte Cassino, Nola, Philippopolis, Constantinople, Chalcedon, Thessalonica, Caesarea, Nisibis, Hispalis, Vivarium, Ephesus, Antiochia, Hippo Regius, Carthage, Salamis, Ctesiphon, Thagaste, Ptolemais, Jerusalem, Bethlehem, Alexandria, Wadi Natrun, Scetis, Thebes, Adulis, Axum

ATLANTIC OCEAN, Rhine, Dnieper, Caspian Sea, Danube, Black Sea, Mediterranean Sea, Tigris, Euphrates, Syrian Desert, SAHARA, Red Sea, Nile, to southern India

Legend
- early monastic community up to the 6th century A.D.
- capital of Diocletianic diocese
- spread of Christianity
- Christian communities around 100 A.D.
- largely Christian by the 6th century

0 — 800 km
0 — 500 mi

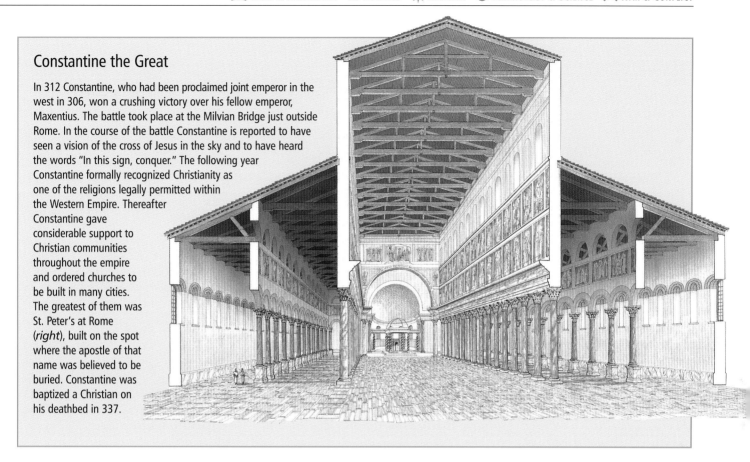

Constantine the Great

In 312 Constantine, who had been proclaimed joint emperor in the west in 306, won a crushing victory over his fellow emperor, Maxentius. The battle took place at the Milvian Bridge just outside Rome. In the course of the battle Constantine is reported to have seen a vision of the cross of Jesus in the sky and to have heard the words "In this sign, conquer." The following year Constantine formally recognized Christianity as one of the religions legally permitted within the Western Empire. Thereafter Constantine gave considerable support to Christian communities throughout the empire and ordered churches to be built in many cities. The greatest of them was St. Peter's at Rome (*right*), built on the spot where the apostle of that name was believed to be buried. Constantine was baptized a Christian on his deathbed in 337.

☀ **c.67** Paul is executed in Rome.

☀ **c.95** The Emperor Domitian resumes the persecution of Christians.

☀ **197** Tertullian, a Roman soldier's son converted to Christianity, writes his *Apology*, arguing that Christians can be trusted as good citizens.

☀ **222** All persecution of Christians temporarily ceases under the rule of the Emperor Alexander Severus.

☀ **250** The Emperor Decius renews the persecution of Christians. Fabian, the 20th pope (bishop of Rome), is martyred.

☀ **252** Cyprian, bishop of Carthage in North Africa, holds a council of bishops that reaffirms the pope's position at the head of the Christian Church.

▶ Diocletian, seen here with his three imperial coregents, was a fierce persecutor of the early Christian Church.

☀ **303** The Emperor Diocletian unleashes a violent persecution of Christians across the Roman Empire.

☀ **c.305** St. Anthony founds colonies of hermits in the Egyptian desert.

☀ **312** Constantine adopts the symbol of the cross at the Battle of the Milvian Bridge.

☀ **c.319** The theologian Arius propounds his theory of the Trinity, which argues that God the Son is not equal with God the Father.

☀ **325** Constantine presides over the first General Council of the Church, held at Nicaea, which condemns Arius's views as a heresy.

☀ **405** St. Jerome completes the first Latin translation of the Bible.

☀ **c.430–460** St. Patrick preaches Christianity in Ireland.

☀ **451** The Eastern Emperor Marcian calls the Council of Chalcedon; more than 500 bishops attend.

☀ **c.480** St. Benedict is born at Nursia, near Spoleto in Italy. The Benedictine rule he will devise for his monastery at Monte Cassino, dividing the monk's day into set periods for work and prayer, will become the model for monastic life in western Europe.

AMERICAS

411 According to Mayan inscriptions, Tikal is the dominant Mayan city during the reign of King Stormy Sky (–457).

c.450 With an estimated population of 200,000 people and covering an area of 8 square miles (20 sq. km), Teotihuacán is at the peak of its influence in central Mexico.

c.500 The ceremonial site of Moche, in the Moche Valley of northern Peru, is abandoned after heavy flooding; the associated Moche Culture begins to decline.

EUROPE

402 Ravenna, on the Adriatic coast of Italy, replaces Rome as the capital of the Western Empire.

407 Britain ceases to be part of the Western Empire after the Roman garrison is withdrawn.

408 Stilicho is executed on the orders of the Western Emperor Honorius on trumped-up charges of treason.

410 Alaric leads a Visigoth army to sack Rome.

413 Theodosius II builds a strong defensive wall to protect Constantinople.

c.450 Groups of Anglo-Saxons, originally from northern Germany and Denmark, begin to settle in eastern and southern England.

455 Pope Leo the Great negotiates a peace with the Vandals after they attack Rome.

475 Julius Nepos, the last legitimate western emperor, is driven out of Italy by a palace coup; Romulus Augustulus, a young boy, is made emperor in his place.

476 Romulus Augustulus is deposed by Odoacer, a barbarian general who declares himself king of Italy, thus marking the end of the Roman Empire in the west.

c.480 Boethius, statesman and author of the *Consolations of Philosophy*, one of the most widely read books of the Middle Ages, is born.

AFRICA

c.400 Jenné-Jeno, in present-day Mali, has grown by this date into a city with defensive walls; at the southern end of the caravan routes across the Sahara, it is a flourishing center of trade.

415 Hypatia, a mathematician and philosopher of Alexandria, is murdered by a Christian mob, perhaps on the instructions of Cyril, archbishop of Alexandria, who resented her influence.

429 A Vandal army crosses from Spain to North Africa.

WESTERN ASIA

409 The Sassanian Emperor Yazdigird issues an edict allowing Christians in Persia to worship openly; he later rejects it and authorizes the persecution of Christians once again.

455 The Persians suppress Christianity in Armenia, now a Persian province, and forcibly convert the population to Zoroastrianism, the Persian state religion (–456).

484 The Sassanian ruler Peroz is killed while campaigning in the east against the White (Ephthalite) Huns.

SOUTH & CENTRAL ASIA

c.400 A new group of nomads, the Juan-Juan, now control the oasis towns at the eastern end of the Silk Road.

5th-century Hindu sculpture of the god Vishnu in the form of a boar.

414 The death of Chandragupta II ends further expansion of the Gupta Empire in India.

c.415 From this time on the Guptas' northwest border is increasingly threatened by the Huns.

EAST ASIA & OCEANIA

c.400 Indian traders introduce Hinduism to parts of Southeast Asia.

c.400 Polynesian seafarers settle the Hawaiian Islands.

407 The Juan-Juan repeatedly invade China's northern frontier (to 449), but are repulsed by the Wei state.

427 King Changsu moves the capital of Koguryo (Korea) to Pyongyang.

439 The state of Wei now controls all of northern China.

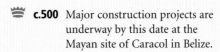
👑 **c.500** In the Andes a new state, Huari, emerges to the north of Tiahuanaco, with which it will compete for control of lowland trade.

👑 **c.500** Major construction projects are underway by this date at the Mayan site of Caracol in Belize.

AMERICAS

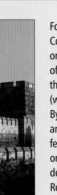

Founded in 330 A.D. by the Emperor Constantine, Constantinople was built on the site of the existing settlement of Byzantium to serve as the capital of the eastern half of the Roman Empire (which in later years would become the Byzantine Empire). The city grew in size and importance as the Western Empire fell apart, and in 413 Theodosius II ordered the building of new land defenses that almost doubled its size. Recently restored, the Theodosian walls are shown at left.

✕ **486** Clovis, king of the Franks, defeats a Roman general at Soissons and begins the southern expansion of his kingdom.

✕ **489** Theodoric, king of the Ostrogoths, defeats Odoacer and takes control of Italy (–493).

☀ **491** Possible date of Clovis's conversion; he is baptized as a Catholic.

EUROPE

✕ **431** The Vandals capture the Roman town of Hippo after a siege during which St. Augustine, bishop of Hippo and one of the greatest leaders of the early Christian Church, dies.

✕ **439** The Vandals capture Carthage and make it their capital.

✕ **468** A Byzantine fleet, sent to reconquer Africa from the Vandals, is destroyed off Cape Bon, Tunisia.

AFRICA

👑 **484** Persia's new ruler, Balas, agrees to pay tribute to the White (Ephthalite) Huns.

☀ **498** Balas's successor Kobad is forced to abdicate the throne because of his support for Mazdak, a Zoroastrian high priest who preaches an extreme form of the religion.

WESTERN ASIA

✕ **c.460** The Gupta King Skandagupta defeats an invasion of White (Ephthalite) Huns from Central Asia.

☀ **c.500** Rock-cut temples at Ajanta, central India, are painted with religious frescoes at this time.

Buddhist wall painting from Ajanta, India.

SOUTH & CENTRAL ASIA

☀ **c.450** By this time 90 percent of the population of northern China is Buddhist.

✕ **c.500** The Kingdom of Champa in central Vietnam takes advantage of Chinese weakness to launch crossborder raids.

EAST ASIA & OCEANIA

400–500 CE   **43**

THE FALL OF THE ROMAN EMPIRE

IN 476 A.D. A GERMAN GENERAL *named Odoacer overthrew the last Roman emperor in the west, thereby ending nearly 500 years of imperial rule. The collapse of the empire was not sudden or unexpected. The threat to Rome had been building up for years as the weakened Roman army faced increasing pressure from beyond its borders.*

▲ In the late 3rd century A.D. the Emperor Diocletian made a valiant but short-lived attempt to restore the fortunes of the declining empire. This bust of Diocletian comes from Nicomedia in Asia Minor (Turkey), where he established his headquarters.

▶ In the 5th century the Roman Empire's western half fell apart, divided up between invading peoples. Its eastern lands remained mostly intact as the core of the Byzantine Empire, which survived for another 1,000 years.

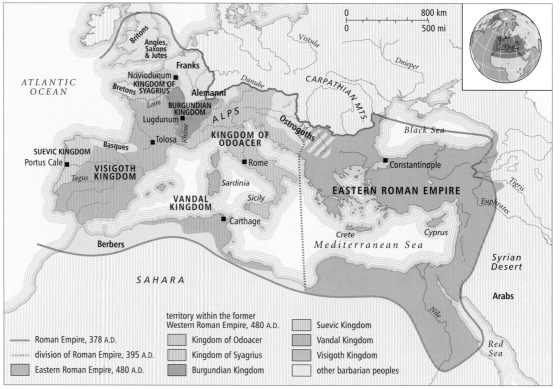

Roman Empire, 378 A.D.
division of Roman Empire, 395 A.D.
Eastern Roman Empire, 480 A.D.

territory within the former
Western Roman Empire, 480 A.D.
Kingdom of Odoacer
Kingdom of Syagrius
Burgundian Kingdom

Suevic Kingdom
Vandal Kingdom
Visigoth Kingdom
other barbarian peoples

224 A.D. Rome loses one foreign rival when the Parthian kingdom comes to an end, only to be confronted by a new one: the Parthians' conquerors, the Sassanian rulers of Persia.

231 Emperor Alexander Severus launches a first campaign against the Sassanians.

235 A chaotic period begins in which power rests with the army; in all, 37 different men are declared emperor over the next 35 years, although many fail to win the supreme office.

240 For the first time the empire finds itself attacked on several fronts: in Africa, in Europe, and in Persia.

256 The Franks take advantage of the withdrawal of a Roman garrison from Gaul to cross the Rhine frontier into the empire.

260 The Emperor Valerian is seized by the Sassanian Emperor Shapur while attempting to negotiate a truce. He ends his life in Persian captivity.

269 Claudius II wins a great victory over the Goths at the Battle of Naissus, taking the title of Gothicus.

c.280 The Romans build a series of strongholds known as the Saxon Shore forts to protect the coasts of Britain and Gaul from pirate raids.

284 Diocletian comes to power and sets about restoring the authority of the emperors.

286 Diocletian splits control of the empire with his friend Maximian. He takes control of the eastern half, giving Maximian authority over the west.

293 Diocletian further subdivides control over the empire, establishing the Tetrarchy (rule of four), under which two separate *augusti* (rulers) share control in each half of the empire.

324 Constantine reunites the empire under one-man rule.

For centuries past the Romans had traded with the Germanic tribes settled beyond the empire's northern frontier. In the 3rd century, however, relations worsened. German raiders, attracted by the empire's wealth, made frequent attacks across its borders. On the eastern frontier, too, the Romans were under military threat from the Sassanian rulers of Persia.

After a century and a half of stability the Roman emperors now found themselves almost constantly at war. No individual could hope to rule without the support of the army, which was frequently withdrawn. In all, 26 emperors ruled between 235 and 284, reigning on average for less than two years each; all but one died violently. The cost of raising armies and defending the frontiers brought financial ruin.

In 284 Diocletian became emperor. He decided that the empire was too large to be ruled by one man and divided it into eastern and western halves, placing each half in the charge of two *augusti*, or co-emperors. He also doubled the size of the army. As a result of these measures, taxes rose, forcing farmers to leave the land. Famines were frequent, and the population declined, especially in the western half of the empire. A shortage of manpower led the Romans to start recruiting German mercenaries (soldiers fighting for pay) into their armies.

In the late 4th century the Huns burst out of Central Asia to ravage the lands to the west of the Black Sea, establishing a kingdom in Hungary. Their devastating raids

The Huns

The Huns who exploded out of Central Asia into Europe in the 4th and 5th centuries have earned one of the most fearsome reputations in history—their name is still used to invoke extreme savagery. Their war leader Attila was known as "the scourge of God." Under his leadership the Huns swept through the Balkans, defeating the Emperor Theodosius II in three battles and threatening the walls of Constantinople. In 451 the Huns invaded Gaul, but a combined army of Romans and Visigoths defeated them at the Battle of Châlons, and Attila retreated to Hungary. He led one further invasion into Italy, but died in 453. Deprived of his leadership, his empire quickly collapsed.

caused widespread panic among the German tribes, who fled for safety across the Roman frontier. The Romans had no resources to hold back the waves of invaders, and in the course of the next century the Germans carved out kingdoms for themselves in Gaul, Spain, North Africa, and Italy. The eastern half of the Roman Empire clung on to survive for another millennium as the Byzantine Empire, but by 500 A.D. all traces of Roman authority had vanished from western Europe.

▶ Romans gave the name "barbarians" to the tribal peoples who lived beyond their borders and did not share their culture. This mounted Germanic warrior clutching a lance and shield was carved on a tombstone in the 7th century A.D.

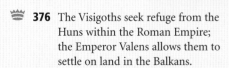

✕ **376** The Visigoths seek refuge from the Huns within the Roman Empire; the Emperor Valens allows them to settle on land in the Balkans.

✕ **378** The Visigoths rebel and kill Valens at the Battle of Adrianople.

✕ **406** A barbarian army of Vandals, Suevi, and Alans crosses the Rhine and invades deep into Gaul.

✕ **c.435** The Roman general Aetius uses Hun mercenaries against the Burgundians and other Germanic tribes settled in Gaul.

✕ **441–451** The Huns invade the empire.

✕ **451** Aetius defeats Attila's army in Gaul.

✕ **455** A Vandal army crosses from North Africa to sack Rome.

👑 **476** Odoacer declares himself king of Italy and is recognized by the Eastern Emperor Zeno.

👑 **480** Julius Nepos, the last legitimate western emperor, dies.

👑 **488** Zeno encourages the Ostrogoth leader Theodoric to invade Italy.

👑 **493** Odoacer is murdered, and Italy becomes part of the Kingdom of the Ostrogoths.

FACTS AT A GLANCE

Achaean League
An alliance of most of the city-states of Greece, formed in about 275 B.C. It managed to defeat Sparta, but was itself defeated by the Romans in 146 B.C.

acropolis
Literally "high city," the fortified citadel of a Greek city-state.

Actium, Battle of
A naval battle (31 B.C.) in which Octavian defeated the fleet of Mark Antony and Cleopatra off the western coast of Greece.

Adena Culture
A group of North American hunter–gatherer communities that settled in the Ohio River valley from about 1000 B.C. The culture was at its peak from approximately 700 to 100 B.C.; finds from sites include copper jewelry and decorated human skulls.

Aeneid
Epic poem by Virgil relating the founding of Rome through the legend of Aeneas, a Trojan prince who, following the fall of Troy, wanders the Mediterranean before settling in Italy.

Aeschylus
c.525–c.456 B.C. The first great Greek dramatist.

Agrippa
63–12 B.C. Roman general who commanded the victorious fleet at the Battle of Actium. Agrippa married Emperor Augustus's daughter and was heir apparent to the imperial throne before his death.

Alans
A nomadic tribe that established itself in southeast Russia in the first three centuries A.D. Under pressure from other nomads one group of Alans moved west to Spain.

Alexander the Great
356–323 B.C. King of Macedon and conqueror of the Persian Empire, Alexander was the most successful soldier of the ancient world, carrying Greek culture to Egypt, West and Central Asia, and northern India. His vast empire collapsed in the Wars of the Diadochi soon after his death.

Alexandria
City on Egypt's Mediterranean coast founded by Alexander the Great.

Anasazi Culture
A farming and hunter–gatherer culture in the North American Southwest. Early Anasazi lived in houses sunk into the ground around larger buildings that may have been used as religious centers.

Anatolia
The Asiatic part of Turkey, known in Roman times as Asia Minor.

Anglo-Saxons
Germanic peoples (Angles, Saxons, and Jutes) who migrated to Britain from Germany and Denmark from about 450 A.D. on and established a number of kingdoms there. In time the Anglo-Saxons became known as the English.

Antiochos I
c.323–261 B.C. Seleucid ruler of Syria, son of one of Alexander the Great's generals.

Antiochos III
242–187 B.C. King of Syria and Asia Minor who restored Seleucid power in Armenia and Persia. He invaded Greece to recover lost territories but was defeated by the Romans, who were determined to have no rivals in the Mediterranean.

Archimedes
c.287–212 B.C. Greek mathematician and inventor, born at Syracuse in Sicily. During the Second Punic War Archimedes designed machines for the defense of Syracuse but was killed when the Romans stormed the city.

Ardashir I
King of Persia (reigned c.208–240 A.D.) who defeated his Parthian overlords in 224 and founded the Sassanian Dynasty.

Aristotle
384–322 B.C. Greek philosopher and scientist who became tutor to Alexander the Great in 342. On returning to Athens, he set up his own school at the Lyceum.

Arius
c.250–336 A.D. Christian theologian who believed that Christ was not divine but was the first and highest of all created things. Arianism, based on his teachings, was condemned at the Council of Nicaea (325) but nevertheless had many adherents, especially in the Eastern Roman Empire.

Armenia
An ancient country occupying the mountainous region of western Asia between the Black Sea and the Caspian Sea, Armenia became allied to the Roman Empire in 69 B.C. In 303 A.D. it became the first country to adopt Christianity as a state religion.

Aryans
Nomadic pastoralists from Central Asia who migrated into the Indian subcontinent around 1500 B.C. They introduced Sanskrit, the language of the earliest Hindu scriptures.

Ashoka
The greatest of the Mauryan rulers of India (reigned c.269–232 B.C.), who was a convert to Buddhism.

Asia Minor
The Asiatic part of present-day Turkey, also known as Anatolia.

Attila
War leader of the Huns (434–453 A.D.). Attila brought scattered groups of warriors together into a fearsome army that overran much of the Roman Empire from the Balkans to Gaul until defeated by a Roman–Visigoth army.

Augustus
The title taken by Octavian when he became the first Roman emperor in 27 B.C.

Aurelian
Roman emperor from 270–275 A.D., Aurelian was a successful military commander who did much to restore the fortunes of the empire.

Axum
A powerful trading kingdom in northeastern Ethiopia. From the 1st century A.D. up to the Byzantine era Axum traded with Greeks, Romans, Arabs, and Indians.

Ayurveda
A Hindu medical system developed by c.50 B.C.

Babylon
Capital of ancient Babylonia, on the bank of the Euphrates River in what is now Iraq; by 500 B.C. it had become part of the Persian Empire.

Bactria
Ancient country in what is now northern Afghanistan. Part of the Persian Empire in 500 B.C., it was conquered by Alexander the Great in 328 B.C. On his death it became part of the Hellenistic Seleucid Kingdom until about 250 B.C.

Ban Chiang Culture
A farming culture in northeast Thailand. By about 300 B.C. the Ban Chiang people were producing printed textiles and pottery that was often painted with images of humans, animals, and insects.

baptism
The rite of admittance into the Christian church by symbolic cleansing with water.

barbarian
Term used by the Romans to denote all peoples living outside the frontiers of the Roman Empire, but in particular the Germanic-speaking peoples settled on its northern frontiers.

basilica
A Roman public building used as law courts or offices. The building consisted of a large hall flanked by columns with an aisle on each side; the design was adopted by early Christians for their churches.

Basketmaker Culture
A society of the early Anasazi Culture that had no pottery but used baskets and other woven artifacts.

bodhi
In Buddhism a term meaning enlightenment or spiritual awakening.

Bodhidharma
Indian Buddhist (born c.470 A.D.) credited with bringing Buddhism to China. His form of Buddhism, called Chan, became Zen Buddhism in Japan.

bodhisattva
A person who by his or her good deeds is free to enter the state of perfect serenity called *nirvana* but who, out of compassion for all living things, remains in the world to work for the salvation of others.

Boudicca
British queen of the Iceni tribe of the East Anglia region who led a revolt against the Romans after they seized her lands and raped her daughters. Her forces burned London and other cities before being defeated. Boudicca then poisoned herself.

Buddha
"Enlightened one," the name applied to Siddhartha Gautama, founder of Buddhism.

Caesar, Julius
c.100–44 B.C. Roman general, politician, and writer. After conquering Gaul, he defied the Senate to lead his army to Rome in 49 B.C. Victor in the civil war that followed, Caesar was declared dictator for life in 44 B.C. but was assassinated in the same year.

Caligula
12–41 A.D. Roman emperor who succeeded Tiberius in 37 A.D. A cruel and mentally unstable tyrant, Caligula was assassinated by an officer of his personal guard.

Cannae, Battle of
One of Rome's worst military defeats. In 216 B.C. Carthaginian troops led by Hannibal encircled and destroyed an entire Roman army in central Italy.

Caria
An ancient region on the coast of southwest Asia Minor that was an independent kingdom under King Mausolus (c.377–353 B.C.).

Carthage
A great maritime trading city founded by the Phoenicians near modern Tunis on Africa's north coast. Destroyed by the Romans during the Punic Wars, Carthage was rebuilt as a Roman colony in 45 B.C.

catacomb
A network of underground burial chambers.

Catholic
A member of the Christian church recognizing the authority of the pope in Rome.

Celts
Iron Age peoples of Europe sharing a common culture and related languages, called *keltoi* by the Greeks and Gauls by the Romans. From the 5th century B.C. on, bands of Celts invaded Greece and Italy. Others migrated into western Europe as far as Spain and the British Isles.

Champa
Also known as Lin-yi Champa. Kingdom founded about 192 A.D. on the central and southern Vietnamese coast. Its language, culture, and religion were shaped mainly by trade with Hindu India.

Chandragupta I
King of Magadha from 320 to 335 A.D. who founded the powerful Gupta Dynasty.

Chandragupta II
Indian king of the Gupta Dynasty from 380 to 414 A.D. He fought a long campaign against the Sakas and extended the Gupta Empire into northern India and the Deccan Plateau.

Chandragupta Maurya
Indian king from about 321 to 290 B.C. and founder of the Mauryan Dynasty. He created a great empire on the Ganges Plain of northern India and extended its borders to the Indus Valley in the northwest.

Characene
A kingdom at the head of the Persian Gulf, near modern Basra in Iraq, which served as a trading center between the Roman Empire and the east.

Chavín de Huantar
Site in northern Peru that was an important cult center from about 900 to 200 B.C. It has given its name to the Chavín style of art, featuring carved mythical creatures combining feline, serpent, bird, and human characteristics.

Cicero
106–43 B.C. Roman orator, politician, lawyer, and writer. He opposed Mark Antony's bid for power and was murdered by Antony's agents.

Cisalpine Gaul
The section of the Roman province of Gaul that lay south of the Alps.

city-state
A self-governing city controlling a surrounding area of land, large or small. In ancient Greece a city-state was called a *polis*, from which the English word "politics" derives.

Claudius
10 B.C.–54 A.D. Roman emperor who succeeded Caligula in 41 A.D. Claudius was a scholar and an able administrator who extended the Roman Empire. He was probably poisoned by his fourth wife, the mother of Nero by a previous marriage.

Cleopatra
c.68–30 B.C. Queen of Egypt and mistress first of Julius Caesar and then of Mark Antony. Defeated at the Battle of Actium, Cleopatra killed herself rather than be captured by the Romans.

Colosseum
The largest amphitheater in Rome, 615 feet (187 m) long and 160 feet (49 m) high. It could even be flooded for mock sea battles.

Commodus
161–192 A.D. Roman emperor who came to power in 180. Commodus was a vicious megalomaniac who believed that he was a living god. Fearing that they would be his next victims, some of his close associates had him murdered.

Confucius
551–479 B.C. Celebrated Chinese administrator and philosopher, known in China as Kongfuzi. His teachings, emphasizing learning, respect, and good conduct, became a state religion in China.

Constantine the Great
c.267–337 A.D.; Roman emperor from 312 A.D. Brought up at the imperial court, he succeeded his father as co-emperor of the western provinces (Britain, Gaul, and Spain) in 306, then defeated all other rivals to become western emperor in 312 and sole emperor in 324. He issued the Edict of Milan (313) extending toleration to Christians, and was baptized on his deathbed.

consul
One of two annually elected officials who exercised supreme civil and military authority during the Roman Republic. After the establishment of the empire the office became purely honorary.

Cyprian, Saint
Born about 200 A.D., Cyprian was bishop of Carthage, North Africa, and was executed during the anti-Christian persecutions of Emperor Valerian in 258.

Dacia
A kingdom north of Rome's Danube frontier in modern Romania. Conquered by the Romans in 106 A.D., Dacia remained a province until 272, when it was abandoned to the invading Goths.

Darius I
King of Persia (c.550–486 B.C.) who sent an expedition against the mainland Greeks to punish them for supporting Ionian cities in revolt against Persian rule but was decisively defeated at the Battle of Marathon (490). He died as he was preparing a second expedition against the Greeks and was succeeded by Xerxes I.

Darius III
Last Achaemenid ruler of Persia (335–330 B.C.), who was defeated by Alexander the Great at the Issus River (333) and Gaugamela (331). After the latter defeat he fled from the scene of battle and was murdered by one of his officers.

diaspora
The dispersal of the Jews following the Roman sack of Jerusalem in 70 A.D. and the crushing of the Jewish revolt of 135.

Diadochi, Wars of the
The wars from 321 to 301 B.C. between Alexander the Great's former generals Ptolemy, Seleucus, Cassander, Antigonus, and Lysimachus, which resulted in the breakup of Alexander's empire (Diadochi is Greek for "successor").

Diocletian
Roman emperor whose administrative and financial reforms helped restore the fortunes of the empire. Born in 245, Diocletian was proclaimed emperor by his troops in 284. He divided the empire into four areas of military responsibility, thereby improving arrangements for its defense, and took the unusual step of abdicating power in 305. He died in 316.

Dong Zhuo
Chinese warlord who seized power from the Han emperor in 189 A.D. He burned the Han capital Luoyang and moved to Changan, where he was murdered in 192.

El Mirador
An early Mayan city in Guatemala, founded in about 400 B.C. It went into terminal decline in the 1st century A.D.

Ephthalite Huns
Also known as the White Huns. A branch of the Huns who overran much of the Sassanian Empire of Persia in the 4th to the 6th centuries A.D. and helped bring about the downfall of the Gupta Dynasty in northern India in about 510.

Epiros
A kingdom in northwestern Greece whose ruler Pyrrhos invaded Italy in 280 B.C. After its failure to conquer Rome a weakened Epiros was attacked by its neighbors. Later imperial Rome established colonies in Epiros.

Eratosthenes
c.276–194 B.C. Mathematician, astronomer, and geographer, born in the Greek city of Cyrene in North Africa, who became the head of the great library of Alexandria in Egypt.

Etruscans
An advanced civilization in Etruria (northern and central Italy) that dominated early Rome. Rome shook off Etruscan rule in 509 B.C., and Etruria was eventually absorbed into the Roman Empire.

Euclid
c.330–260 B.C. Greek mathematician who taught in Alexandria, Egypt. His *Elements*, describing the principles of geometry, is the earliest known Greek mathematical treatise.

Franks
A Germanic people who settled in what is now the Netherlands in the 3rd century B.C. After the fall of the Western Roman Empire the Frankish kings gradually conquered most of Gaul. France is named for them.

Funan
A trading kingdom in what is now Cambodia and southern Vietnam. Funan grew rich on the profits of the seaborne trade between India and China from the 2nd to the 6th centuries A.D.

Galatia
A state in Asia Minor founded in the 3rd century B.C. by Celtic settlers. It became a Roman province in 25 B.C.

Gaul
The region approximating to present-day France and Belgium lived in by the Celts. The Romans gradually conquered all of Gaul between 225 and 51 B.C.

Great Wall of China
A continuous defensive barrier built along China's northern border to protect the settled Chinese people from raiding nomads. About 25 feet (8 m) tall, it is a brick-faced structure of earth and stone with carefully sited watchtowers.

Gupta Dynasty
The dynasty founded by Chandragupta I, king of Magadha, that ruled an empire in northern India from the 4th to 6th centuries A.D. Hindu culture flourished under the Guptas.

Hadrian
76–138 A.D. Roman emperor who succeeded Trajan in 117. Hadrian spent much of his reign in the provinces, strengthening the imperial frontiers. He was also a scholar who established an institute called the Athenaeum to sponsor writers and philosophers.

Hadrian's Wall
A defensive stone barrier built by Hadrian to protect Roman Britain from the tribes of the north.

Hamilcar
c.270–228 B.C. Carthage's most formidable general during the First Punic War. He died in battle in Spain, having made his son, Hannibal, swear undying hatred of Rome.

Han Dynasty
Chinese dynasty that ruled (with one short interval) from 206 B.C. to 220 A.D. Under the Han rulers science and technology made remarkable advances.

Hannibal
247–183 B.C. Carthaginian general who launched the Second Punic War in 218 B.C. He invaded Italy and won several battles but was forced to withdraw to Africa, where he was defeated by the Romans at Zama.

Hasmonean Dynasty
Jewish dynasty founded by a priest called Mattathias (d.166 B.C.), who with his son Judas Maccabeus led the Maccabean Revolt against Seleucid rule. The dynasty survived until 30 A.D.

Hellenistic Period
The period lasting from the death of Alexander the Great in 323 B.C. to the Roman conquest of Egypt in 30 B.C., during which Greek culture was the dominant influence in the eastern Mediterranean and western Asia.

Hermann
Also known as Arminius, the Latin form of his name; c.18 B.C.–17 A.D. Tribal chief who led a German army that cut three Roman legions to pieces in the Teutoburg Forest.

Hero of Alexandria
Greek mathematician who lived in Alexandria in the 1st century A.D. He invented many machines, including a stationary steam engine, a water organ, and a pump for a fire engine.

Herod the Great
74–4 B.C. King of the Roman province of Judea from 40 B.C. Although he was an able ruler, his attempts to impose Greek customs on his Jewish subjects aroused deep hostility.

Herodotus
c. 485–425 B.C. Greek writer regarded as "the father of history," who wrote a pioneering and discursive history of the Greek–Persian wars.

Hinduism
The dominant religion and culture of India since ancient times. A complex system of beliefs and customs, Hinduism includes the worship of many gods and a belief in rebirth.

Hipparchos
c.180–125 B.C. Greek astronomer who, among other achievements, calculated the length of the solar year, estimated the distance of the Earth from the sun, and catalogued more than 1,000 stars.

Hippocrates
c.460–377 B.C. Celebrated Greek physician. Since ancient times the so-called Hippocratic Corpus, a collection of medical and surgical treatises written over a period of 200 years, has been ascribed to him, although he probably wrote only one or two of the works involved.

Hohokam Culture
A farming culture centered on the Gila River in present-day Arizona. To water their fields, the Hohokams dug 300 miles (500 km) of irrigation canals.

Hopewell Culture
A farming culture of eastern North America. From about 100 B.C. the Hopewell constructed massive earthworks as ritual centers.

Huns
Nomadic peoples from Central Asia, one group of whom (known as the Black Huns) migrated to eastern Europe around 370 A.D. and established a kingdom in present-day Hungary. Legendary for their violence, they disappeared from history after the death of their leader Attila in 453. See also Ephthalite Huns.

Ionia
Ancient name for the central west coast of Asia Minor, including some islands of the eastern Aegean Sea. Ionia was named for the Ionians, Greek-speaking peoples who migrated to the region from mainland Greece from the 11th to 9th centuries B.C.

Issus River, Battle of the
Alexander the Great's victory against a much larger Persian army led by Darius III in 433 B.C.

Izapa Culture
A culture associated with Izapa, an archaeological site near Chiapas, Mexico. Its inhabitants may have transmitted the Olmec calendar and religious beliefs to the Maya.

Jainism
A religion founded in India by the 6th century B.C.; it teaches the necessity of self-denial in order to obtain spiritual liberation and urges sympathy and compassion for all forms of life.

Jin Dynasty
Also known as the Western Jin. Shortlived Chinese dynasty set up by Wudi in 265 A.D.

Juan-Juan
An alliance of Central Asian nomads that controlled the northern frontier of China from the early 5th to mid 6th century A.D. They included the Avars, who later harassed eastern Europe.

Judea
Roman province in the southern part of ancient Palestine, formerly the Jewish kingdom of Judah.

Jugurtha
d.104 B.C. King of Numidia (in North Africa) who in 112 revolted against Rome. By bribery, guerrilla warfare, and sheer force of personality he held out for eight years.

Julian calendar
A calendar introduced in 45 B.C. by Julius Caesar. It had 12 months rather than the previous ten; the additional months, July and August, were named for Caesar and Augustus, respectively.

Juvenal
c.60–140 A.D. Roman satirist who used viciously witty poetry to criticize the decadence of Roman society.

Kalinga
An ancient region on the east coast of India in the present-day state of Orissa.

Kanishka
The greatest of the Kushan kings, ruling around 100 A.D., who used Chinese, Parthian, Indian, and Roman titles on his coins to proclaim his kingship.

Koguryo
The earliest Korean state. Arising in the 1st century A.D., it was strongly influenced by Chinese culture. Buddhism was introduced in 372. It was conquered by the neighboring state of Silla in 668.

Kushans
A wealthy dynasty of kings (mid 1st–4th centuries A.D.) who ruled an empire in Afghanistan and northern India that controlled trade along the Silk Road.

Lapita Culture
Ancient Pacific culture named for an archaeological site in New Caledonia. The Lapita people probably came from Southeast Asia, bringing with them domesticated animals and a type of pottery incised with geometric patterns.

La Tène Culture
Iron Age culture associated with the Celts, which takes its name from a prehistoric settlement in Switzerland. The characteristic La Tène art style developed around 450 B.C. and made use of lively animal motifs and intricate geometrical patterns.

Liu Bang
247–195 B.C. Emperor of China who founded the Han Dynasty in 206. Of peasant stock himself, Liu won the affection of ordinary people by his down-to-earth manner, but also took advice from men of learning.

Maccabees, Revolt of the
The struggle for Jewish independence led by the Maccabee family (maccab is Aramaic for "hammerer"), also known as the Hasmoneans. Judas Maccabee took Jerusalem from its Seleucid rulers in 164 B.C., and his brother Simon established Jewish independence in 142.

Macedon
Mountainous kingdom in northern Greece bordering the Aegean Sea. It rose to importance in the 4th century B.C. under Philip II, father of Alexander the Great.

Magadha
One of the 16 kingdoms of northern India mentioned in classical Hindu writings. It was located on the middle Ganges River and formed the heartland of the Mauryan Empire.

Magnesia, Battle of
A Roman victory (190 B.C.) over Antiochos III's Seleucid forces at Magnesia (Manisa in modern Turkey). The turning point in the battle came when Seleucid war elephants stampeded through their own troops.

Mahayana
A school of Buddhism that teaches that the highest ideal is for individuals to work for the salvation of others (see bodhisattva).

Marathon, Battle of
Battle (490 B.C.) fought on the Marathon plain about 26 miles (42 km) north of Athens in which an army of massed Athenian spearmen, led by Miltiades, defeated a much larger Persian force. The Persians lost 6,400 men, the Athenians only 192.

Marcus Aurelius
121–180 A.D. Roman philosopher and emperor (from 161). His reign was marked by constant warfare, plague, and insurrection. These calamities are reflected in his *Meditations*, an influential literary work dominated by thoughts of death.

Mark Antony
82–30 B.C. Roman soldier and politician. After Caesar's death Mark Antony and Octavian split the Roman world between them, with Antony ruling Egypt with his lover, Cleopatra. Rivalry between Mark Antony and Octavian led to war. Decisively beaten at the Battle of Actium, Mark Antony returned to Egypt and committed suicide.

Masada
A rock fortress high above the Dead Sea in Judea where the Jews made their last stand in their revolt against the Romans. After the Romans captured the stronghold in 73 A.D., the defenders committed suicide rather than fall into their hands.

Mauretania
The "land of the Moors," covering coastal Morocco and Algeria. In 44 A.D. the Emperor Claudius divided it into two Roman provinces, but large parts of the country remained under Moorish chieftains.

Mauryan Dynasty
The first north Indian dynasty to extend its rule into central and eastern India. The Mauryan Empire (c.321–180 B.C.) was created by Chandragupta Maurya and enlarged by his son Bindusara and grandson Ashoka.

Maya
Amerindian people of southern Mexico, Guatemala, and Honduras. The Maya of the Classic Period (c.250–800 A.D.) are noted for their stepped pyramids, carved monuments, and knowledge of astronomy. They used a hieroglyphic form of writing.

Menander
Indo-Greek ruler who conquered India as far south as the Ganges. Menander converted to Buddhism.

Mengzi (Mencius)
c.371–289 B.C. Chinese philosopher and sage in the tradition of Confucius. Mencius believed that human nature is innately good, although goodness requires cultivation.

Meroë
Nubian kingdom from about 590 B.C. to 350 A.D. Egyptian influence was strong: The kings and queens of Meroë were buried in pyramids, and inscriptions were carved in a hieroglyphic script, as yet undeciphered.

Messiah
In Jewish prophetic writings the future savior or deliverer. Christians believe that the Messiah came in the person of Jesus.

Milan, Edict of
Imperial proclamation issued in 313 A.D. by Constantine in the Western and Licinius in the Eastern Roman Empire, granting religious toleration for Christians.

Mithridates I
d.138. Parthian ruler who wrested control of much of Persia from the Seleucids.

Moche Culture
The culture associated with the Moche River valley in coastal northern Peru, which flourished from about the 1st to 8th century A.D. The Moche people built ceremonial centers with platform mounds; one of them, the Pyramid of the Sun, is the largest such mound in South America.

Monte Albán
Capital of the Zapotec people, in Mexico's Oaxaca region. Founded around 500 B.C., Monte Albán was the dominant regional center for over 1,000 years.

Mylae, Battle of
A naval battle (260 B.C.) in which the Roman fleet destroyed 50 Carthaginian ships. Instead of ramming the enemy—the Carthaginian tactic—the Romans used grappling devices to immobilize their vessels while soldiers leaped on board.

Nabataea
A kingdom that expanded along the caravan routes radiating from the city of Petra, in modern Jordan. It became the Roman province of Arabia in 106 A.D.

Nazca Culture
A culture that flourished in the southern deserts of Peru from about 370 B.C. to 700 A.D., famed for creating large designs in the desert gravel that sometimes extended for miles. Seen most easily from the air, their purpose remains unknown.

Neoplatonism
A philosophy that sees everything on Earth as a reflection of an eternal divine reality. It developed in the late Roman Empire and remained influential throughout the Middle Ages.

Nero
37–68 A.D. Roman emperor who succeeded Claudius in 54. Nero's murderous oppression of real or imagined opponents alienated the Senate. Forced to flee Rome, he committed suicide.

Nicaea, Council of
The first general council, or gathering, of the Christian church, called by Constantine in 325 A.D. to establish a shared set of beliefs.

nirvana
The end of rebirth and suffering—the ultimate goal of Buddhism. Some see it as the merging of the self with the universe.

Nok Culture
An Iron Age culture that flourished in Nigeria from about 500 B.C. to 200 A.D. Its art is characterized by terracotta sculptures of people and animals.

Nubia
The region to the south of Egypt on the Nile River, roughly equivalent to modern Sudan. The ancient Egyptians called it Kush.

Numidia
The country of the Numidae, covering an area in the north of present-day Algeria and western Tunisia. It became a Roman province in 46 B.C.

Octavian
63 B.C.–14 A.D. Roman general and first emperor of Rome. The adopted son of Julius Caesar, Octavian won a power struggle with Mark Antony and other rivals to become supreme ruler, known as Augustus.

Ostrogoths
A Germanic people living in the area around the Black Sea who were conquered and displaced by the Huns in about 372 A.D. Under their leader Theodoric (c. 455–526), they moved into Italy in 488 and established a kingdom there that lasted until 555.

paganism
Belief in many gods.

Palmyra
An ancient oasis city in the Syrian desert that prospered from its position on the caravan route from the Mediterranean to the Persian Gulf. It became part of the Roman Empire in 18 A.D.

Parthians
A nomadic people from Central Asia who ruled Persia (modern Iran) and Mesopotamia (Iraq) from about 247 B.C. to 226 A.D. The Romans captured the Parthian capital in 115 A.D., but they never succeeded in totally subduing the region.

patricians
A class of Roman citizens descended from the oldest noble families. In early republican times they alone could enter the Senate or hold other high offices.

Peloponnesian Wars
Two series of conflicts (457–445 and 431–404 B.C.) between the city-states of Sparta and Athens, fought mostly in the Peloponnese, the southern peninsula of mainland Greece.

Perdiccas
Macedonian nobleman who became regent to Alexander the Great's infant son in 323 B.C. He struggled to keep Alexander's empire together, but was murdered in Egypt in 320.

Pergamon
Ancient Greek city near the modern Turkish town of Bergama. An ally and then possession of Rome, it became a center of Greek art and culture.

Pericles
c.495–429 B.C. Athenian statesman who dominated the city-state from about 460 and led Athens in the Peloponnesian Wars against Sparta.

Persepolis
The chief royal residence and capital of the Achaemenid Dynasty of Persia, famed throughout the ancient world for its opulent splendor.

Persian Empire
The empire in western Asia created by Cyrus the Great (550–529 A.D.) of the Achaemenid Dynasty. At its height it extended from the Mediterranean Sea to the Indus Valley. It lasted until 331 B.C., when it was conquered by Alexander the Great.

Philip II
Ruler of Macedon from 359 to 336 B.C. who made his kingdom a major military power.

Phoenicians
Seafaring traders, originally from Lebanon, who established a vast commercial empire with its main center at Carthage. The Roman word for Phoenician was *Punicus*, as in Punic War.

Plataea, Battle of
The last land battle of the Persian War, fought in Greece in 479 B.C. A mainly Spartan force decisively defeated Xerxes' army, forcing him to abandon all further ideas of conquering Greece.

Plato
c. 428–347 B.C. Greek philosopher who founded his own school of philosophy, the Academy, in Athens. He was a follower of Socrates and wrote an account of Socrates' trial. His best known work, *The Republic*, outlines his vision of the ideal state.

plebeians
A class of Roman citizens composed of traders and small farmers. The plebeians had their own assembly, but its resolutions became legally binding on the whole population only after 287 B.C.

Plotinus
205–270 A.D. Philosopher, probably born in Egypt of Roman parentage, who studied in Alexandria and Persia before setting up in Rome as a teacher. His writings established Neoplatonism as a philosophical system and greatly influenced early Christian theology.

Plutarch
46–c.120 A.D. Greek writer best known for his *Parallel Lives*, biographies comparing Greek and Roman soldiers and politicians.

Pompeii
An ancient Roman port and pleasure resort near Mount Vesuvius, south of modern Naples. In 79 A.D. Pompeii was completely buried in a volcanic eruption that killed about 2,000 citizens. Its ruins were excavated from 1748 on.

Pompey
106–48 B.C. Roman general and consul. When Julius Caesar marched on Rome in 49 B.C., Pompey was given command of the republican forces opposing him. Defeated in the ensuing civil war, he fled to Egypt, where he was murdered.

Pope
The title given to the bishops of Rome who, claiming descent from St. Peter, from the third century on asserted their leadership of the Christian church.

Ptolemaic Dynasty
The dynasty of pharaohs of Macedonian descent who ruled Egypt from 323 to 30 B.C. The last of the Ptolemies was Queen Cleopatra.

Ptolemy I
c. 367–283 B.C. The founder of the Ptolemaic dynasty of Egyptian rulers, Ptolemy was Macedonian by birth. He was one of Alexander the Great's generals and also possibly his half-brother.

Ptolemy, Claudius
c.90–168 A.D. Egyptian astronomer and geographer who worked in Alexandria. His theory that the Earth was the center of the universe remained largely unchallenged until the 16th century.

Punic Wars
Three wars fought between Rome and Carthage. The conflict began as a dispute over Sicily but became a protracted struggle for control of the whole Mediterranean.

Puranas
Sacred Hindu writings dealing with ancient times and events.

Pyrrhos
King of Epiros in Greece who in 280 B.C. invaded Italy and inflicted two defeats on the Romans. His own losses were so heavy that he was forced to withdraw—hence the phrase "a Pyrrhic victory," meaning a victory achieved at too high a price.

Qin
A Chinese state that unified China in 221 B.C., giving its name to the whole country and to the dynasty that ruled it for the next 15 years.

Qu Yuan
c.340–278 B.C. Chinese statesman and poet who produced most of his poetry during periods of exile from the imperial court. The anniversary of his death is still celebrated in China.

Ramayana
Indian epic poem of about 300 B.C. in which the hero Rama and his friend Hanuman strive to recover Rama's wife Sita, abducted by the demon king Ravana.

Romulus
Legendary founder and first king of Rome, supposedly a descendant of the Trojan prince Aeneas.

Rubicon River
A river separating Italy and the Roman province of Cisalpine Gaul. Provincial governors were not allowed to return to Rome without permission, so when Julius Caesar led his army across the Rubicon in 49 B.C., he knew it would lead to civil war. Hence "to cross the Rubicon" means to take an irrevocable step.

Saba
An ancient country, known as Sheba in the Bible, roughly equivalent to present-day Yemen in southwest Arabia. Saba's wealth was based on its control of the caravan trade in incense, aromatic resins valued throughout the ancient world for use in religious ceremonies and as a component of perfumes and cosmetics.

Sakas
Nomads from Central Asia who invaded Afghanistan and eastern Persia from about 170–130 B.C. and established a kingdom in northwestern India around 94 B.C.

Salamis, Battle of
Naval battle (480 B.C.) between the Greeks and the Persians off the island of Salamis in the Bay of Eleusis west of Athens.

Samnites
An ancient people of central Italy who were conquered by the Romans in a series of wars between 343 and 290 B.C.

Samudragupta
Second in the line of Gupta kings (reigned 335–380 A.D.), he established Gupta power across northern India.

Sanskrit
The dominant classical language of India and the sacred language of Hinduism.

Sassanians
Also known as Sassanids. Dynasty of Persian kings (224–651 A.D.) named after Sassan, grandfather of Ardashir I, the first Sassanian ruler.

Scipio Africanus
"African Scipio," 237–c.183 B.C. Roman general who defeated the Carthaginians in Spain, invaded Africa in 204, and defeated Hannibal at Zama in 202.

Scythians
Nomads from Central Asia who migrated into the region north of the Black Sea during the 8th and 7th centuries B.C. They traded with the Greeks and were conquered by Philip II of Macedon in 339 B.C.

Seleucid Dynasty
The dynasty founded by Seleucus I that ruled much of Asia Minor, Mesopotamia, and Syria during the Hellenestic period from 321 to 64 B.C.

Seleucus I
c.358–280 B.C. A general in Alexander the Great's army, Seleucus proved to be the most ambitious of his successors. He succeeded in establishing a large kingdom for himself in the east, but was murdered by a Ptolemy rival when he appeared to have designs on Egypt.

Senate
Rome's governing council. In early republican times the Senate was composed of about 80 patricians. At the end of the republic there were about 600 senators, drawn from all classes of society. Under imperial rule the Senate's powers were greatly reduced.

Seneca
c.4 B.C.–65 A.D. Roman philosopher and playwright. He was tutor to the future Emperor Nero, but lost favor after Nero came to the throne and was ordered to commit suicide.

Severus, Septimius
Roman emperor (ruled 193–211) who waged a successful campaign against the Parthians. He died at York after putting down a rebellion in Britain.

Shang Yang
390–338 B.C. A philosopher and minister of Qin who introduced a repressive law code designed to direct the whole energies of the state to farming and war.

Shapur I
A Sassanian king (ruled 240–272 A.D.), the successor of Ardashir I, who won territory from the Armenians and Kushans.

Shihuangdi
The title, meaning "first emperor," adopted by the Qin warrior-king Ying Sheng after he unified China.

Shu
The westernmost of the three kingdoms of China after the fall of the Han Dynasty in 220 A.D. The other two were Wei and Wu.

Shunga Dynasty
A short-lived Hindu dynasty (c.182–172 B.C.) that persecuted Buddhists.

Siddhartha Gautama
c.563–483 B.C. A Nepalese prince who gave up his privileged existence, followed an austere way of life, practiced meditation, and became the founder of Buddhism.

Silk Road
Ancient overland trade route extending for roughly 4,000 miles (6,400 km) between China and Europe.

Sima Qian
c.145–87 B.C. Chinese historian and court astrologer who wrote the first official history of China—a task begun by his father.

Social War
A three-year uprising by Rome's Italian allies, who demanded full Roman citizenship. In 88 B.C. Rome agreed to their demands. The creation of new Roman communities led to the development of urban centers throughout Italy.

Socrates
469–399 B.C. One of the greatest figures of Greek philosophy, Socrates established the "Socratic method," which sought to establish the truth of ideas through questioning and dialogue.

Sogdiana
A northeastern province of the Persian Empire (in present-day Uzbekistan) conquered by Alexander the Great between 329 and 327 B.C.

Sohano Period
A cultural period (c.200 B.C.–600 A.D.) in the Pacific characterized by pottery with geometric decoration. It probably developed from the Lapita Culture.

Sophocles
c.496–405 B.C. Greek tragic dramatist. His seven major surviving plays include *Antigone* and *Oedipus Rex*.

Spartacus
A gladiator from Thrace who in 73 B.C. led a slave revolt that laid waste to much of southern Italy. Defeated in 71 B.C., Spartacus was crucified.

stele
A stone monument (plural stelae) carved with sculptured images or inscriptions, usually commemorating a ruler's achievements.

Strabo
c.60 B.C.–20 A.D. Greek geographer and historian who traveled widely gathering information for his *Geographica*, a description of the known world.

Suevi
One of a number of Germanic peoples displaced by the Huns. They established a kingdom in Spain in 409 A.D. that was later absorbed into the Visigoth Kingdom.

Tacitus
c.55–120 A.D. Roman historian who wrote the *Annals* and *Histories*, two accounts of the Roman empire covering the years 14–68 and 68–96 A.D. respectively.

Talmud
The most important work of post-Biblical Jewish literature, containing Jewish law and tradition.

Teutoburg Forest, Battle of the
A rare and costly defeat for Rome. In 9 A.D. three Roman legions marching back to winter quarters in Germany were ambushed and annihilated by Germanic tribesmen led by Hermann in dense forest near the modern town of Osnabrück.

Theravada
A school of Buddhism that emphasizes the meditative way of life as the way for individuals to attain *nirvana*.

Thermopylae, Battle of
Battle of the Greek–Persian Wars. Thermopylae is a narrow pass between mountains and sea in central Greece. In 480 B.C. a small Spartan army held it for three days against Xerxes' much larger invasion force, allowing time for the rest of the Greek army to escape, but were all killed themselves.

Thrace
A country formed of parts of modern Greece, Bulgaria, and European Turkey. Conquered by Philip of Macedon in 342 B.C., it was later incorporated into the Roman Empire.

Tiahuanaco
A city close to Lake Titicaca in Bolivia that was the center of an Andean empire from about 300 to 700 A.D.

Tiberius
42 B.C.–37 A.D. Roman emperor who succeeded Augustus in 14 A.D. His rule began well, but degenerated into tyranny, with a growing number of treason trials and executions.

Tiberius Gracchus
168–133 B.C. Roman tribune who tried to change the way land was distributed to the poor. He was opposed by the Senate (whose members were the main landowners), and in 133 he and 300 supporters were murdered.

Tikal
The largest Maya city in the lowland region of Guatemala during the Classic Period (300–800 A.D.).

Titus
39–81 A.D. Roman emperor who succeeded Vespasian in 79. Titus captured Jerusalem in 70. As emperor, he ruled with fairness and generosity.

Toba
Nomads who conquered northern China in 386 A.D. and established a dynasty in the state of Wei.

Trajan
52–117 A.D. Roman emperor who came to power in 98. Trajan's conquests of Dacia and Parthia marked the high point of the Roman Empire.

tribune
An official elected by the plebeians to protect their interests. When the position was created in 494 B.C., two tribunes were elected annually; later this number was increased to ten.

Trojans
People of Troy, an ancient city thought to have occupied a site at Hisarlik, close to the mouth of the Dardanelles strait in modern Turkey. According to the Greek poet Homer, Troy was destroyed by the Greeks after a long siege.

Teotihuacán
Ancient city in the Valley of Mexico about 30 miles (50 km) north of Mexico City. At its height (c.300–600 A.D.) it had a population of around 150,000 and covered a larger area than ancient Rome.

Twelve Tables
The first Roman code of laws, inscribed on stone in 451 B.C. Until the end of the republic schoolboys had to learn them by heart.

Valerian
Roman emperor (ruled 253–260). He was taken prisoner by the Sassanians after the Battle of Edessa (260) and died in captivity.

Vandals
A Germanic people who invaded the Roman Empire between 406 and 409 A.D. and settled in Spain. In 429 they reached North Africa and established a kingdom there from which they attacked Rome in 455. The Vandal Kingdom survived until 534.

Veii
An Etruscan city about 12 miles (19 km) north of Rome, which was captured by Rome in 396 B.C. after a ten-year siege.

Vespasian
9–79 A.D. Roman emperor who restored order after the succession struggle known as the Year of the Four Emperors. He reformed the administration, put the empire's finances in order, and began an extensive program of public building.

Visigoths
A Germanic people, related to the Ostrogoths, who invaded the Roman Empire in the 4th century and founded a kingdom in southern France and Spain.

Wang Mang
45 B.C.–25 A.D. Chinese emperor who seized the Han throne in 9 A.D. His reforms to improve the life of peasants were undermined by famine and other natural disasters. His murder by rebels restored the Han Dynasty to power.

Warring States Period
Period of Chinese history from 481–221 B.C., when the authority of the Zhou emperors was in disarray and power was in the hands of a few major states almost constantly at war with one another.

Wei
The northernmost, as well as the richest and most populous, of the three kingdoms of China after the collapse of the Han Dynasty in 200 A.D.

Wu
In the south of China one of the three kingdoms of China after the collapse of the Han Dynasty.

Wudi
The name taken by two seperate Chinese emperors. One ruled from about 141 to 87 B.C. during the Han Dynasty. The other established the short-lived Jin Dynasty in about 265 A.D.

Xerxes I
c.519–465 B.C. Ruler of Persia (reigned 486–465 B.C.) who tried to conquer Greece in 480 but was defeated at the battles of Salamis and Plataea.

Xiongnu
A Central Asian tribe of nomads who posed a constant threat to the Chinese Empire. The Xiongnu were probably the Huns who invaded the Roman Empire in the 5th century A.D.

Yamato Kings
The rulers of the Yamato Plain on Honshu Island, who gradually extended their authority throughout the whole of Japan between the 4th and 8th centuries A.D. They were strongly influenced by Chinese culture.

Yayoi Culture
Japan's first rice-farming and metalworking culture. Mirrors and coins at Yayoi sites indicate that Japan at the time had contacts with Han China.

Year of the Four Emperors
A bloody succession struggle following the death of Nero. Between June 68 and January 69 three emperors—Galba, Otho, and Vitellius—briefly held power. All died violently.

Yellow Turbans
Chinese rebels, mainly poor peasants, who began a two-year revolt against Han corruption in 184 A.D. They were led by three magicians.

Zama, Battle of
Crucial Roman victory over the Carthginians. In 202 B.C. a Roman army under Scipio Africanus defeated Hannibal in present-day Algeria, bringing the Second Punic War to an end.

Zapotecs
A people of ancient Mexico living in the Oaxaca Valley region. They developed the earliest script in the Americas around 800 B.C., and their most important center was at Monte Albán, which flourished between 400 B.C. and 700 A.D.

Zenobia
Queen of Palmyra from 266 to 272 A.D. She came to power after the murder of her husband Odenathus and led an uprising against the Roman Empire after declaring her son emperor in the east in 270. She was defeated by the Emperor Aurelian and taken to Rome to be exhibited, covered in jewels, in his victory parade.

Zhou Dynasty
China's longest-lasting imperial dynasty, which held power from 1122 to 256 B.C.

Zoroastrianism
Religion founded by the Persian prophet Zoroaster (or Zarathrusta) that sees the world in terms of a struggle between the forces of good and evil. It is still practiced by a few communities in Iran and by the Parsis of western India.

Further Reading

Adkins, Lesley and Roy A. *Handbook to Life in Ancient Rome*. New York, NY: Facts on Focus, 2004.

Basham, A.L. *The Wonder that was India: A Study of the History and Culture of the Indian Sub-Continent before the Coming of the Muslims*. New York, NY: Hawthorn Books, 1963.

Boardman, John, Jasper Griffin, and Oswyn Murray, eds. *The Oxford History of the Roman World*. New York, NY: Oxford University Press, reprint edn., 2001.

Brown, Peter R.L. *The Rise of Western Christendom*. Malden, MA: Blackwell, 2nd edn., 2003.

Brown, Peter R.L. *The World of Late Antiquity*. New York, NY: W.W. Norton & Company, 1989.

Burger, Richard L. *Chavín and the Origins of Andean Civilization*. New York, NY: Thames & Hudson, reprint edn., 1995.

Carrithers, Michael. *The Buddha*. New York, NY: Oxford University Press, 1989.

Cotterell, Arthur. *The First Emperor of China: The Greatest Archeological Find of Our Time*. New York, NY: Holt, Rinehart, & Winston, 1983.

Cunliffe, Barry. *Greeks, Romans, and Barbarians: Spheres of Interaction*. New York, NY: Methuen, 1988.

Davidson, Ivor J. *The Birth of the Church: From Jesus to Constantine A.D. 30–312*. Grand Rapids, MI: Baker Books, 2004.

Demand, Nancy. *A History of Ancient Greece*. Boston, MA: McGraw Hill, 1996.

Ferrill, Arther. *The Fall of the Roman Empire*. New York, NY: Thames & Hudson, reprint ed., 1988.

Grant, Michael. *The Routledge Atlas of Classical History*. London: Routledge, 5th edn., 1995.

Gray, Basil, ed. *The Arts of India*. Ithaca, NY: Cornell University Press, 1981.

Gernet, Jacques. *A History of Chinese Civilization*. Cambridge, UK: Cambridge University Press, revised edn.,1996.

Grant, Michael, ed. *Roman Readings*. Baltimore, MD: Penguin Books, 1958.

Green, Peter. *Alexander to Actium: The Historical Evolution of the Hellenistic Age*. Berkeley, CA: University of California Press, reprint edn., 1993.

Hammond, N.G.L. *The Miracle that was Macedonia*. New York, NY: St. Martin's Press, 1991.

Holland, Tom. *Rubicon: The Last Years of the Roman Republic*. New York, NY: Doubleday, 2003.

Hopper, R.J. *The Early Greeks*. New York, NY: Barnes & Noble, 1977.

Hornblower, Simon. *The Greek World 479–323 B.C.* New York, NY: Routledge, 3rd edn., 2002.

Hucker, Charles O. *China's Imperial Past: An Introduction to Chinese History and Culture*. Stanford, CA: Stanford University Press, 1994.

Kagan, Donald. *The Peloponnesian War*. New York, NY: Viking, 2003.

Kenyon, Kathleen, and S. Moorey. *The Bible and Recent Archeology*. Atlanta, GA: John Knox Press, revised edn., 1987.

Lane Fox, Robin. *Alexander the Great*. New York, NY: Penguin Books, 2004.

Scullard, H.H. *A History of the Roman World 753–146 B.C.* New York, NY: Routledge, 5th edn., 2002.

Scullard, H.H. *From the Gracchi to Nero: A History of Rome from 133 B.C. to A.D. 68*. New York, NY: Routledge, 5th edn.,1990.

Strassler, Robert B., ed. *The Landmark Thucydides: A Comprehensive Guide to the Peloponnesian War*. New York, NY: Free Press, 1996.

Syme, Ronald. *The Roman Revolution*. New York, NY: Oxford University Press, revised edn., 2002.

Webster, Graham. *The Roman Invasion of Britain*. New York, NY: Routledge, revised edn., 1999.

Wells, Peter S. *The Battle that Stopped Rome*. New York, NY: W.W. Norton & Co., 2003.

Set Index

Volume numbers are in **bold**. Page numbers in **bold** refer to main articles; those in italics refer to captions.

100 Days Movement **9**:47
1812, War of **9**:8, *9*
Abbas I of Persia **6**:*39*, 43, **7**:6, **8–9**, 15
Abbas II of Persia **7**:23, 31
Abbasid Dynasty **3**:23, *25*, 28, 29, 36, 48 **4**:34, 46
Abd al-Aziz **8**:31
Abd al-Aziz ibn Saud **10**:6, 7
Abdali **8**:10, 46
Abdallah ibn Faisal **9**:38, 43
Abd al-Malik **3**:20, 21, 22
Abd al-Mumin **4**:26, 30
Abd-el-Kader **9**:29
Abdul Aziz **9**:30, 38
Abdul Hamid I **8**:34, 38
Abdul Hamid II **9**:38, 39, 40, 43, **10**:6, 8
Abdul Mejid **9**:20
Abdurrahman III **3**:40
Abelard, Peter **4**:23
Aborigines **1**:10, **8**:*41*, 46
Abu al-Qasim **8**:26

Abubakar II **5**:14, 16, 17
Abu Bakr **3**:16, 19, 22, 23
Abu Hayan **5**:15
Abu'l Hasan **6**:37
Abu Said **5**:15
Abu Zakaria Yahya I **4**:42
Acadia **7**:18, 46, **8**:7, 10, 46
Acamapichtli **5**:26
Aceh **6**:46, **7**:22, 46
Achaean League **2**:46
Achaemenid Dynasty **1**:38, 46
Achille Lauro **10**:40
Achitometl **5**:14
Acolhua **5**:6
Acre **4**:20, 21, **5**:8, 9, 10, 11
Actium, Battle of **2**:46
Adams, John **8**:43, 9:6
Adams, John Quincy **9**:14
Adams, Will **7**:20–21
Aden **6**:46, **9**:19
Adena Culture **1**:26, *38*, 46, **2**:46, **4**:46
Aditya I **3**:37
Adrianople, Treaty of **9**:15
Aegospotami **2**:9
Aemilianus, Scipio **2**:19
Aeschylus **2**:8, 46

Aetius **2**:45
Afghani, al **9**:41
Afghanistan **3**:44, **8**:23, **9**:8, 28, 30, 34, 39, **10**:30, 39, 44, *46*
Afghan Wars **9**:20, 21, 28, 39, 48
Afonso I of Kongo **6**:23
Afonso Henriques **4**:27
Agadir Incident **10**:8
Agaja **8**:14, 19
Age of Discovery **5**:44–45
Agha Muhammad **8**:43
Aghlabid Dynasty **3**:29, 33, 48
agriculture, development **1**:8–9, 10, 16, *17*, 18
Agrippa **2**:28, 46
Agung **7**:15
Ahab (king of Israel) **1**:31, 46
Ahmad Gran **6**:18, 19, 22, 23, 46
Ahmad ibn Ibrahim al-Yasavi **4**:31
Ahmad Shah Durrani **8**:*22*, 23, 26, 31, 46
Ahmed I **7**:6, 11
Ahmed III **8**:6, *7*, 10, 18
Ahmed al-Mansur **6**:38
Ahmose **1**:19, 24, 25, 46
Ahuitzotl **5**:42
Aidan, St. **3**:17
AIDS **10**:39, 48

Ainu people **3**:29
Aix-la-Chapelle, Treaty of **7**:32, **8**:23, 29
Ajanta **2**:*43*
Ajanta Caves **9**:13
Ajnadyn, Battle of **3**:19
Akbar **6**:27, 30, 31, 34, 35, 36, *37*, 38, 39, 42, **7**:*10*, 38
Akhenaten (Amenhotep IV) **1**:22, 24, *25*, 46
Akkadian Empire **1**:15, 46
Ala al-Din Husayn **4**:30
Ala al-Din Muhammad **4**:35
Alaca Höyük **1**:14, 46
Alamo **9**:*18*, 19
Alaric II **3**:8
Alaska **9**:31
Alauddin **4**:36
Alaunngpaya **8**:26
Albany Congress **8**:27
Albert of Hapsburg **5**:35
Alberti, Leon Battista **5**:38
Albigensian Crusade **4**:42
Albigensians **4**:20, 21, 29, 39, 46
Albuquerque **8**:7
Albuquerque, Afonso de **6**:8, 10, 11
Alcatraz Island **9**:46
Alembert, Jean d' **8**:16, 17

Aleppo **5**:35, **9**:7
Alexander II of Russia **9**:30, 40
Alexander III of Russia **9**:40, 46
Alexander the Great **2**:10, 11, **12–13**, 32, 46
Alexander Nevsky, St. **4**:*43*
Alexandria, Egypt **2**:10, 11, *13*, 22, *32*, 33, 34, 46, **3**:19
Alexis I **4**:19, **7**:27
Alfonso I of Aragon **4**:23
Alfonso VI of Castile **4**:19
Alfred the Great **3**:*37*, 39
Algeria **5**:22, **9**:15, 18, 24, 28, 29, **10**:27, 28, *29*
Algiers **3**:41, **6**:11, 15, 34, **8**:30, **9**:6, 29
Ali (Muhammad's son-in-law) **3**:20, *22*, 23
Ali Bey **8**:34
Allende, Salvador **10**:35
Alliance, Treaty of **8**:35, 53
All India Muslim League **10**:7
Allouez, Claude Jean **7**:31
Almeida, Francisco de **6**:6, 7, 8
Al Mina **1**:46
Almohads **4**:22, 26, 27, 30, 35, 38, 39, 46 **5**:6, 46
Almoravids **4**:11, 15, 18, 19, 22, 46
Alp Arslan **4**:15, 16, 17
alphabets **1**:34, 40, **5**:35
Alqas Mirza **6**:23
Alsace **9**:35, **10**:13
Altan Khan **6**:35
Alvardi Khan **8**:22
Alvarez, Francisco **6**:14
Amangkurat I **7**:23
Amasya, Treaty of **6**:26, 53
Amazon River **5**:43
Amda Siyon **5**:14
Amenemhet I **1**:24
Amenhotep I **1**:19, 46
America
 peopled **1**:6–7
 Spanish rule **8**:20–21
American Civil War **9**:30, 31, **32–33**
American Revolutionary War **8**:21, 34, **36–37**, 38, 46
Amin, Idi **10**:35, 39
Amina **5**:14, **7**:10
Amorites **1**:18
Amritsar **6**:*35*, **9**:8, **10**:13, 40
Amsterdam **6**:8, **7**:36, 37
Anabaptists **6**:19, 46
Anasazi Culture **2**:26, 46, **3**:16, 32, 48, **4**:22, 26, *32*, *33*, 35, 46, **5**:10, 46
Anatolia **2**:12, 46, **3**:40, **5**:33, 39, 46, **6**:26, 46, **7**:46, **8**:46
Anawrahta **4**:11, 24, 25
Andagoya, Pascual de **6**:15
Andalusia **4**:43, 46
anesthetics **9**:21
Anga Chan **6**:26
Angelico, Fra **5**:35
Angkor **3**:16, 33, **4**:15, 24, 25, 34, 46, **5**:46, **6**:46,
Angkor Empire **5**:11, 14
Angkor Thom **4**:34
Angkor Wat **4**:23, *24*, 25, 46 **6**:26
Anglo-Burmese Wars **9**:25, 26, 28, 41
Anglo-Dutch Wars **7**:*26*, 30, 36
Anglo-French Treaty **9**:47
Anglo-French War **6**:22, 23, 26
Anglo-Saxons **2**:42, 46 **3**:*16*, 17, 48, **4**:46
Anglo-Sikh Wars **9**:21, 24, 48
Angola **6**:13, 38, 43, **7**:15, 22, 46, **8**:22, **10**:27, 38
animals, domestication **1**:8, *9*, 14, 15
Annam **3**:40, 41, 48, **5**:42, **9**:40
Anne of England **8**:11
An Qing **2**:30
Anselm, St. **4**:11

Anson, George **8**:23
Antarctica **10**:29
Anthony, St. **2**:35, 41
Anti-Comintern Pact **10**:21, 48
Antioch **4**:19, *21*, 31, **5**:8
Antiochos III **2**:14, 15, 18, 46
Antiochos IV Epiphanes **2**:18, 32
Antoninus **2**:29
Antony, Mark **2**:23, 25, 50
Antwerp **6**:8, 9, 35, **7**:37
Anuradhapura **2**:7
apartheid **10**:38, 48
Aphilas **2**:35
Aquino, Benigno **10**:40
Aquino, Corazon **10**:41
Arab–Israeli wars **10**:25
Arab League **10**:22, 48
Arabs **3**:24, 28, 29
 astronomy **3**:33, 37, 44, **4**:6
 conquests **3**:16, 17, 19, 20, 21, 22, 25
Arafat, Yasser **10**:35, 44, 46, 47
Arameans **1**:26, 27, 46
Archaic period, Greek **1**:35, 46
Archangel **6**:38
Archimedes **2**:14, 46
Arcot **8**:22, 46
Argentina **9**:12, 15, 16, **10**:28
Arius **2**:41, 46
Ark of the Covenant **1**:*29*, 46
Armada, Spanish **6**:26, *40*, 45, 46
Armenia **2**:38, 42, 46 **4**:14, 38
Armenians **9**:46, **10**:12
Artaxerxes II **2**:7
Artaxerxes III **2**:10
artesian wells **4**:26
Arthur, *King* **3**:9, 32, *33*, 48 **4**:29
Aryabhata **3**:9
Aryans **1**:18, 19, 22, 26, 46, **2**:46
Asaf Jah **8**:14
Ashanti **7**:34, 46, **8**:6, 18, 22, 46, **9**:14, 31, 35, 48, **10**:6, 48
Ashanti Wars **9**:35, 46, 48
Ashikaga Shogunate **5**:19, **6**:15, 31, 46
Ashoka **2**:15, 20–*21*, 36, 46
Ashraf **8**:18
Ashurbanipal **1**:38
Askiya Dynasty **5**:42
Assassins **4**:*17*, 18, 26, 41, 46
Assurdan II **1**:27
Assyrians **1**:22, 23, 25, 27, 28, 29, 30, 31, 34, *35*, 38, 46
astrolabes **3**:45, **5**:*44*, 46, **7**:*11*, *44*
astronomy, Chinese **2**:22, **3**:41, **4**:8
Astyages **1**:42, 43
Aswan High Dam **10**:28, *29*
Atahualpa **5**:37, **6**:17, 18
Athabascans **5**:10
Athens **1**:31, 38, 42, 43, **2**:6, 8–*9*, 22
atoms, splitting **10**:18
Attalos I **2**:19
Attila **2**:45
Augsburg, Peace of **6**:25, 27, 51
Augustine, St. **2**:43, **3**:13
Augustus (Octavian) **2**:23, *28*
Augustus II (the Strong) **8**:18
Aum Shinri Kyo cult **10**:46
Aurangzeb **6**:*37*, **7**:11, 26, *27*, 30, 31, 34, 35, 38, 39, **8**:6
Aurelius, Marcus **2**:29, 50
Austerlitz, Battle of **9**:7, 10
Australia **7**:43, **8**:34, **9**:6, 12, 24, 27, 30, 31, **10**:6
 gold **9**:25, *40*, 44
 settled by Europeans **8**:39, **40–41**, **9**:15, 18
Austria, Duchy of **4**:29
Austria-Hungary **9**:31

Austrian Succession, War of the **8**:22, 23, 25, 29, 53
automobiles **9**:37, 41, **10**:10–*11*
Ava, Kingdom of **7**:10, 46
Avars **3**:12, 13, 21, 48
Avebury **1**:14, *15*, 46
Averroës (Ibn Rushd) **4**:27
Avicenna **3**:44, *45*, **4**:6, 10
Avignon, papacy at **5**:15
Avilés, Menéndez de **7**:12
Axayacatl **5**:38
Axum **2**:26, 31, *39*, 46, **3**:12, 17
Ayn Jalut, Battle of **4**:41, **5**:7, 8, 9
Ayodhya 45
Ayurveda **2**:23, 46
Ayutthaya **4**:46, **5**:22, 46, **6**:23, 30, 31, 46, **7**:26, 46, **8**:30, 46
Ayyubid Dynasty **4**:30, 43, **5**:6, 7, 46
Azerbaijan **7**:11, 46
Azore Islands **5**:44
Aztecs **4**:39, 42, 46, **5**:11, 14, 22, 26, 34, **36–37**, 38, 42, 46, **6**:7, 46
 account of **6**:35
 Cortés and **5**:37, **6**:11, 14, *16*, *17*

Bab, the **9**:24
Babbage, Charles **9**:13, **10**:42
Babur **5**:28, **6**:*6*, 7, 10, 14, 15, 36, 37, 39
Babylon and Babylonians **1**:18, 28, 29, 31, *38*, 39, 43, 46, **2**:7, 34
Bach, Johannes Sebastian **8**:15
Bacon, Roger **6**:44
Bactria **2**:*18*, 19, 36, 46
Baghdad **3**:23, 28, 45, **4**:14, 41, **5**:27, 31, 38, **7**:9, **8**:6, 19
 Mongols and **5**:7, 8, 28, *29*
 Ottomans and **6**:18, **7**:18, **8**:6
Bahadur Shah **8**:*10*
Baha'i faith **9**:25, **10**:7, 48
Bahama Islands **8**:35
Bahmani Sultanate **5**:30, *31*, 34, 38, 46
Bahrain **9**:39, **10**:17
Bahram **3**:13
Bahri Dynasty **5**:9, 46
Baird, John Logie **10**:18
Bajirao I **8**:18
Bakong **4**:25
Bakri, al- **4**:15
Baku **6**:35
Balban **5**:10
Balboa, Vasco Nuñez de **6**:8, 9, 10
Balearic Islands **1**:38, **4**:38
Balfour Declaration **10**:13
Bali nightclub bombing **10**:47
Balkan Wars **10**:9, 48
Balliol, John **5**:10, 11
Baltimore **8**:15
Banda Bahadur **8**:7, 10, 46
Bandaranaike, Sirimavo **10**:29
Bangkok **9**:*25*
Bangladesh **10**:34, 35, 44
Ban Kao Culture **1**:18, 46
Bantam **7**:6, 39, 46
Bantu **3**:20, 48, **9**:19
Bapheus, Battle of **5**:14
Barakzai Dynasty **9**:18
Barbados **9**:12
Barbarossa **6**:*15*, 19, 22, 28, 29, 46
bar Kokba, Simeon **2**:33
Barnard, Christiaan **10**:33
barometers **7**:44
Barquq **5**:27, 28
Basil I **3**:7, 36
Basil II **3**:7, **4**:6
Basketmaker Culture **2**:*26*, 47
Basra **6**:22, **7**:31, **8**:35
Bastille, stormed **8**:*38*, 39, 45, 46

Batán Grande **3**:36
Batavia **7**:11, 36, 46, **8**:32, *33*, 46
Batavian Republic **8**:43, 46
Baton Rouge, Battle of **8**:21
Battani, al- **3**:37
battery, first **9**:6
Batu **4**:43
Baybars **5**:7, 8, 9
Bayeux Tapestry **4**:*13*, 17, *28*
Bayezid I **5**:27, 29, 30, 33, 42, 43
Bayezid II **6**:7, 10
Bayinnaung **6**:*26*, 27, 30, 31
Bayon **4**:25
Bay of Pigs invasion **10**:32, 48
Beaker People **1**:10, *11*, 14, 46
Beccaria, Cesare **8**:17
Becket, Thomas **4**:*30*, 31
Bede **3**:25
Beethoven, Ludwig van **9**:*14*
Beijing **9**:27
Beirut **10**:40
Bela III **4**:31
Belgrade **8**:19
Belisarius **3**:6, 7
Benedict, St. **3**:*8*, 9
Benedictines **2**:41, **3**:48
Bengal **6**:46, **7**:46, **8**:32, 46, **9**:38, **10**:6
Ben-Gurion, David **10**:*24*
Benin **4**:46 **5**:14, 46, **8**:11, *14*, 46
Berbers **3**:24, 25, 46, **4**:6, 48, **5**:6, 46
Bering, Vitus **8**:15, 22
Berlin Academy of Sciences **8**:25
Berlin Wall **10**:30, *44*
Bernard of Clairvaux **4**:27
Bernard, St. **4**:22
Bernoulli, Daniel **8**:19
Bhamanid Dynasty **5**:19
Bhutan **7**:15, 46
Bhutto, Benazir **10**:41, 44
Biafra **10**:*33*, 34
Bible **2**:41, **5**:26, 40, *41*, **6**:24, *25*, **7**:10
Bihar **5**:43
Bikini Atoll **10**:24
Bill of Rights **8**:37, 42, 46
Bimbisara **1**:43, **2**:6
Biruni, al- **3**:44, **4**:11
Bi Sheng **4**:8
Bismarck, Otto von **9**:30, *31*, 35, 43
Black Death **5**:19, **20–21**, 46, **8**:14, 46
Black Monday **10**:40
Black September **10**:35
Black Sheep Turkmen **5**:26, 31, 34, 38
Blainville, Joseph Céloron, sieur de **8**:23
Blair, Tony **10**:46
blast furnace **8**:19
Blenheim, Battle of **8**:6, 7
Blériot, Louis **10**:*8*
Blood River, Battle of **9**:*20*, 21, 28
Bloody Sunday **10**:7
Blue Mosque **7**:7
Boccaccio, Giovanni **5**:21, 22
Bocskay, Istvan **7**:7
Boers **6**:13, **9**:*18*, 19, 21, 25, 26, 29, 42, *47*, 48
Boer Wars **9**:39, 40, 42, 43, 48, **10**:6, *7*, 48
Boethius **2**:42, **3**:9
Bolívar, Simón **9**:13, *16*, 17
Bolivia **9**:19, **10**:20
Bolsheviks **10**:6, 12, *13*, 48
bombs
 atom **10**:21, *23*, 24, 35
 hydrogen **10**:25, 33
Bonampak **3**:28, *29*, 35
Boniface, St. **3**:25
Boniface VIII, *Pope* **5**:11, 14
Book of the Abacus **4**:38
Book of Hours **5**:*30*
books, earliest printed **3**:36

Boone, Daniel **8**:*34*, 35
Boris I **3**:36
Borobodur **3**:32, **9**:*9*
Bosnia **9**:38, **10**:45, 46
Boston **7**:12, 18, **8**:34
Boston Tea Party **8**:36
Bosworth Field, Battle of **5**:42
Botticelli, Sandro **5**:42, **6**:20
Boudicca (Boudicea) **2**:27, 47
Bougainville, Louis-Antoine **8**:*31*
Bounty **8**:39
Bourbon Dynasty **6**:39, 46
Bourguiba, Habib **10**:35
Bouvines, Battle of **4**:39
Boxer Rebellion **10**:6, 48
Boyle, Robert **7**:44
Boyne, Battle of the **7**:42
Brahe, Tycho **6**:34
Brahmanas **1**:30, 47
Brahmin priesthood **1**:22, 26, 47
Brahmo Samaj **9**:15
Brazil **6**:26, **8**:*13*, 26, **10**:15
    the Dutch and **7**:15, 18, 26
    the Portuguese and **6**:8, 16, 17, 18, 23,
        30, **7**:18, 22, 26, 43
Breda, Treaty of **7**:30
Brennus **2**:10
Brétigny, Peace of **5**:22
Britain
    Iceni tribe **2**:27
    Romans and **2**:23, 25, 26, 42, 44
British Guiana **9**:9
bronze **1**:14, 21, 22, 26, 34, *44*, *45*, **5**:30
Bronze Age **1**:47
Bronzino, Agnolo **6**:19
Brown, John **9**:27, 32
Bruce, James **8**:34
Bruce, Robert **5**:11, 15
Brunel, Isambard Kingdom **9**:*22*, 23
Bruno, Giordano **7**:6
Buddha (Siddhartha Gautama) **1**:42, 43, **2**:6,
    20, 47
Buddhism, growth **2**:*20–21*, 23, 30, 34, 39,
    43, **3**:12, 21, *26*, **4**:6, 24, 46, **6**:47
Buenos Aires **9**:*17*
Bukhara **9**:34
Bulgaria **3**:21, **4**:7, 34, **8**:31, **10**:8
Bulgars **3**:20, 21, 28, 32, 48, **4**:46
Bunker Hill, Battle of **8**:37
Bunyan, John **7**:35
Bureau of Indian Affairs **9**:14
Burji Dynasty **5**:9, 39, 46
Burkina Faso (Upper Volta) **9**:9, **10**:13, 18
Burmans **4**:24
Burr, Aaron **9**:7
Bursa **5**:18
Burton, Richard **9**:42
Burundi **10**:46
Bush, George **10**:41
Bush, George W. **10**:47
Buyids **3**:23, 41, 48, **4**:17, 47
Byzantine Empire **2**:*44*, 45, **3**:6–7, 12, 20,
    32, 40, **4**:6, 13, 31, 34, 47 **5**:14, 27, 46
    6:47
    and iconoclasm **3**:*24*, 25, 28

cables, transatlantic **9**:23, 30
Cabot, John **5**:43, 44, *45*
Cabot, Sebastian **6**:9
Cabral, Pedro **5**:44, **6**:6, 8, *9*, 16
Cádiz **8**:22
caesarean birth **6**:6
Caesar, Julius **2**:*22*, 23, *24*, 25, 49
Cahokia **4**:14, 23, 32, *33*, 43, 47, **5**:14
Cairo **3**:19, *37*, 44, **4**:7, 30
caissons **8**:19
calculators **2**:22
Calcutta **7**:42, **8**:18, *33*, **9**:9
    Black Hole of **8**:26

Caleb **3**:8
calendars **1**:10, 11, 15, **2**:23, **3**:18, 34, *35*,
    4:*21*, **6**:38
California **9**:*24*, 25
Caligula **2**:29, 47
Calvinism **6**:*24*
Calvin, John **6**:22, 24, *25*
Cambodia **3**:*36*, 37, **5**:22, 26, **7**:22, 27,
    10:38
Cambrai, League of **6**:7, 50
Cambyses **1**:25, 42, 43
camellias **8**:19
Camoes, Luis de **6**:34
Camp David Accord **10**:38, 39, 49
Canaan **1**:22, 47
Canada **8**:39, **9**:12, 19, 20, 27, 31
Canary Islands **5**:42
Cannae, Battle of **2**:15, 47
cannons **5**:15, **6**:*44–45*
Cano, Sebastian del **6**:8, *9*, 14, 15
Canterbury Tales **5**:26, *27*
Canyon de Chelly **4**:22, 47
Cape Colony **8**:43, 47, **9**:7, 9, 19, 21, 23,
    28, 42, 43, 44, 48
Capetian Dynasty **3**:45, 48, **5**:46
Cape Town **7**:27
Caracol **2**:43, **3**:12, 35
caravanseries **4**:22
Cárdenas, Lázaro **10**:20
Carmelites, Discalced **6**:30
Carnatic War **8**:23, 47
Carolina, North and South **7**:47, **8**:15
Carolingian Dynasty **3**:48, **4**:47
Carrera, Rafael **9**:20
Cartagena **8**:20, 22
Carter, Jimmy **10**:38
Carthage **1**:30, 47, **2**:10, 18, 19, 22, 24, 25,
    43, 47, **3**:21, 48
Carthaginians **1**:42, **2**:7
Cartier, Jacques **6**:18, *19*
carts, wheeled **1**:13, *21*
Casa Grandes **5**:6
castles, medieval **6**:*45*
Castro, Fidel **10**:28, 29
Catalan Revolt **7**:27, 47
Cateau-Cambrésis, Treaty of **6**:27, 53
Catherine I of Russia **8**:8, 15
Catherine II (the Great) **8**:17, 29, *30*, 43
Catherine de Medici **6**:25, *30*
cathode ray tubes **10**:18
Catholic League **6**:15, 47, **7**:16
cats **1**:15
Ceaucescu, Nicolae **10**:44
Celsius, Anders **8**:22
Celts **1**:27, 31, 39, 40, 47, **2**:14, 15
    La Tène culture **2**:6, 7, 47
ceramics **1**:14
Cervantes, Miguel de **7**:7, 10
Chaco Canyon **3**:40, 49, **4**:26, 30, 32, 47
Chaco War **10**:17, 20, 49
Chaghri-Beg **4**:16, 17
Chalcedon, Council of **2**:41
Chalukya Dynasty **3**:16, 49, **4**:34, 47
Chambord, Chateau of **6**:20, *21*
Champa **2**:31, 43, 47, **3**:16, 49 **4**:25, 34, 47,
    5:38, 47
Champlain, Samuel de **7**:6, *7*, 12
Chan **7**:22, 27
Chancellor, Richard **6**:32
Chan Chan **3**:44, **4**:26, **5**:22, 39
Chandella Dynasty **3**:32, *33*, 49 **4**:26, 31, 34
Chandragupta I **2**:37, 38, 47
Chandragupta II **2**:36–37, 39, 42, 47
Chandragupta Maurya **2**:11, 14, 36, 47
Chang'an **3**:28
Chang Ssu-Hsun **3**:44
Channel Tunnel **10**:45
Chapultepec **5**:11
Charcas **6**:27

Chardin, Jean **7**:34
Charlemagne **3**:29, **30–31**, **4**:44
Charles V, *Holy Roman emp.* **6**:10, *11*,
    14, 15, 17, 18, 22, 27
Charles VI, *Holy Roman emp.* **8**:10, 19
Charles I of Great Britain **7**:15, *28*, *29*
Charles II of Great Britain **7**:29, 30, 44
Charles III of France **4**:29
Charles IV of France **5**:18
Charles VII of France **5**:34
Charles IX of France **6**:30
Charles X of France **9**:14, 15
Charles III of Spain **8**:20–21, 27
Charles XII of Sweden **7**:42, *43*, **8**:7
Charles of Anjou **5**:7, 10
Charles the Bold **5**:42
Charles Edward Stuart **8**:23
Charles the Fat **3**:37
Charles Martel **3**:*11*, 25
Charonea, Battle of **2**:11
Charter 77 movement **10**:38, 49
Chartists **9**:19, 48
Chaucer, Geoffrey **5**:26, *27*
Chavin culture **1**:22, *27*, 34, 47 **2**:6, 11, 18, 47
Chávin de Huantar **1**:30
Cheng Tung **5**:35
Chenla **3**:12, 49
Chernobyl **10**:41
chess **3**:9
Chiang Kai-shek **10**:14, *15*, 16, 21, 24
Chiangmai **6**:26, 47
Chiao Wei-Yo **3**:45
Chicago **7**:34
Chichén Itzá **3**:35, 37, 44, 49, **4**:34, 39
Childeric III **3**:28
Chile **9**:16, 19, 41, 45, **10**:8
Chimú **3**:44, 49, **4**:26, *27*, 38, 47, **5**:*22*, 23,
    37, 39, 42,47
China
    Buddhism **2**:20, 21, 30
    Confucius's **1**:10, **44–45**
Chinese Exclusion Act **9**:40
Chioggia, Battle of **5**:26
Chittor, fortress **6**:37
chivalry **4**:*20*, 21, 31, 47
chocolate **6**:39, **7**:11
chocolatl **5**:22, 47
Chola Dynasty **3**:37, 44, 49, **4**:7, 10, *11*, 15,
    47, **5**:47
Chola State **3**:36
Cholula **3**:15, 25, 49, **4**:18
Choson Dynasty **5**:26, 47
Chrétien de Troyes **4**:29, 31
Christian II of Denmark and Norway **6**:14
Christian IV of Denmark **7**:15, 16
Christianity, spread of **2**:39, **40–41**, **3**:13, 21
Christodoulos **4**:10
chronometer **8**:18
Chulalongkorn **9**:35
Churchill, Winston **10**:22, 30
Cicero **2**:47
Cicilia **5**:26, 47
cinema **10**:*18*
circulatory system **7**:15, 44
circumnavigation, first **6**:8, 15
Cistercians **4**:19, 26, 47
Civil Rights Act **10**:32, 33
Cixi **9**:*38*, 47, **10**:8
Clairvaux **4**:22
Claudius **2**:26, 29, 47
Claudius II **2**:44
Clement, VII, *Pope* **6**:7, 24
Cleopatra **1**:25, **2**:22, 23, 25, 47
Clinton, Bill **10**:45, 46
Clive, Robert **8**:26, *27*, 29, 32
clocks **4**:8, 19, *19*, **7**:36
Clontarf, Battle of **4**:6
Clovis **2**:43, **3**:8, 10–*11*
Cnut (Canute) **3**:39, **4**:7, *10*, 11

Coatlinchan **5**:6
Cobá **5**:30
Cochin China **9**:27, 28, 29, 30, 48
coelacanths **10**:21
Coercive Acts **8**:36, 47
coffee **5**:34, **8**:14
Cold War **10**:30–31, *40*
Colombia **1**:43, **9**:16, **10**:6
colonialism **6**:47, **9**:28–29
    end **10**:26–27
    see also Scramble for Africa
Colosseum **2**:29, 47
Columba, St. **3**:13
Columbus, Christopher **5**:42, 43, 44, *45*, **6**:16
Commodus **2**:31, 47
Commune **9**:35, 48
compasses **2**:27, **4**:11, 18
computer age **9**:13, **10**:*42–43*
Concorde airliner **10**:34, *35*
concrete **2**:18
Confucianism **3**:33, 49, **6**:47, **9**:48
Confucius **1**:*42*, 44, 45, 47, **2**:7, 47
Congo, Democratic Republic of **10**:49
Congo, Republic of **10**:29, 34
Congo Free State **9**:40, 42, 48, **10**:6, 8
conquistadors **5**:37, 47, **6**:9, 11, 14, **16–17**, 22
Conrad II **4**:44
Conrad III **4**:20, 27, 44
Conrad IV **5**:6
Constance, Council of **5**:31
Constance, Peace of **4**:45
Constantine **2**:*38*, 39, 40, *41*, 44, 47
Constantine IV **3**:21
Constantine VI **3**:29
Constantine VII **3**:7
Constantine IX **4**:*15*
Constantine IX Palaeologus **5**:32
Constantinople *see* Istanbul
Constantinople, Treaty of (1479) **5**:42
Constantinople, Treaty of (1784) **8**:38
Constitution, U.S. **8**:*37*, 39
Cook, James **8**:31, *34*, 35, *40*, *41*
Coolidge, Calvin **10**:15
Copán **3**:9, 21, 33
Copernicus, Nicolaus **6**:20, *22*, 23, **7**:44, 47
copper **1**:18, 21
Córdoba **3**:28, 33, **4**:10, 11
Córdoba, Francisco de **6**:11
Corinth **1**:31, **2**:18
corn **1**:10, 26
Corn Laws **9**:22, 48
Cornwallis, Charles **8**:38
Coronado, Francisco **7**:12
Coronado, Vázquez de **6**:22
Corsica **1**:40
Cortenuova, Battle **4**:45
Côrte-Real, Gaspar de **6**:6
Cortés, Hernàn **5**:9, 11, 14, *16*, *17*
Cosmas Indicopleustes **3**:8
Cossacks **7**:22, 27, 34, 40, 41, 47, **8**:47
Coxinga **7**:27, 31, 47
Cranmer, Thomas **6**:27
Crassus **2**:25
Crécy, Battle of **5**:19
Crete **1**:19, **3**:32, **7**:27, 31, **9**:30, 46, **10**:8
    see also Minoans
Crimea **6**:47, **8**:38, 47
Crimean War **9**:*26*, 27, 49
Croatia **10**:45
Croesus **1**:42, 43
Cromwell, Oliver **7**:22, *23*, 28–29
crossbows **2**:*10*
crusader states **4**:22, **5**:*9*, 11
Crusades **4**:19, **20–21**, 26, 27, 35, 38, 39,
    42, *43*, 48, **5**:6, 47
Ctesiphon **2**:31, 34
Cuba **6**:10, 16, **9**:34, 46, 47, **10**:28, 29, 31

Cuban Missile Crisis **10**:30, 31, 49
Cuello **1**:23
Cuicuilco **2**:15, 19
Cultural Revolution **10**:33, 49
Cumberland Road **9**:7
Curie, Pierre and Marie **9**:*46*, 47
currency, paper **3**:33
Curzon, Lord **9**:*46*, 47, **10**:6
Custer, George **9**:38
Cuzco **5**:37, **6**:17
Cyaxares **1**:38, 47
Cyclades **1**:47
Cyprus **5**:34, **6**:34, **10**:35
Cyrus the Great **1**:29, *43*, 47
Cyrus the Younger **2**:7
Czechoslovakia **10**:45

Dacia **2**:30, 48
Dahomey **8**:23, 47
daimyo **5**:38, 42, 47, **6**:31, 47
Dai Viet **5**:38, **6**:18, 47
Dalai Lamas **6**:*34*, 35, 47, **7**:22, 35, 47,
      8:14, 47, **10**:29, 49
Damad Ibrahim Pasha **8**:11
Damalcherry, Battle of **8**:22
Damascus **3**:16, 17, *22*, 24, **4**:27, **5**:28, 30, 35
Damietta **4**:39, 42, *43*
Damiri, al- **5**:23
Dampier, William **7**:43
Dandanqan, Battle of **4**:10
Danegeld **3**:38, 49, **4**:14, 48
Danes **3**:24, 38, 39
Dante Aligheri **5**:14, 15
Dantidurga **3**:29
Daoguang **9**:*13*
Daoism **4**:*8*
Darby, Abraham **8**:19
Darius **1**:43, **2**:6, 9, 48
Darius III **2**:10, 11, 12, 13, 48
Darwin, Charles **9**:18
David (king of Israel) **1**:26, 28, *29*, 47
David, St. **3**:9
David I **5**:27
Davis, John **6**:38
Dead Sea Scrolls **2**:26, *33*
Decameron **5**:21, 22
Deccani Sultanates **6**:31, 47
Deccan region **2**:31, **4**:34, 48, **5**:47, **7**:47,
      8:6, 47, **9**:38
Decembrists **9**:14, 49
Deerfield **8**:7
Defoe, Daniel **8**:11
Delhi **9**:7
Delhi Sultanate **4**:36, *37*, 38, 42, 48, **5**:7,
      11, 15, 22, 26, 27, 30, 47, **6**:15, 47
Demetrius **2**:18
Deng Xiaoping **10**:40
Denkyera, Kingdom of **7**:14, 47
Descartes, René **7**:*19*, 36
Detroit **8**:6
Devaraya II **5**:34
Devolution, War of **7**:32
Dezhnyov, Semyon **7**:23, 41
Dezong **10**:8
Diadochi, Wars of the **2**:48
Diamper, synod of **6**:43
Dias, Bartolomeu **5**:42, 44, *45*
Diaspora, Jewish **1**:29, **2**:*32–33*, 47, 48, **7**:47
Díaz, Porfirio **9**:39
Dickens, Charles **9**:19
Diderot **8**:16, 17, 23
Dien Bien Phu **10**:26, 27
Din-I Ilahi **6**:38, 48
Diocletian **2**:35, 38, 40, 41, *44*, 45, 48, **3**:49
Diogo I of Kongo **6**:26
Ditch, Battle of the **3**:*18*, 19
Diu **6**:19, 23, 48
Divine Comedy, The **5**:14, 15
Diwan **5**:23

Djoser **1**:17, 47
Dmitry, False **7**:7
DNA **10**:*28*
dodo **7**:*38*
Dogen **4**:38
Dolly the sheep **10**:46
Dome of the Rock **3**:*21*, 22
Domesday Book **4**:13, 19, 48
Dominican Republic **9**:21
Dominicans **4**:39, 48, **5**:47
Domitian **2**:41
Donatus **2**:38
Dong Zhuo **2**:31, 48
Don Quixote **7**:7, 10
Dorgon **7**:24, 25
Dorset Culture **1**:34, 47, **4**:48, **5**:31, 47
Dost Mohammad **9**:18, *19*, 20, 30
Draco **1**:39, 47
Drake, Francis **6**:35, 41, 42
Dred Scott case **9**:32
Dreyfus Affair **9**:*45*
Druse (Druze) **4**:48, **8**:10, 47, **10**:15, 49
Dunama Dubalemi **4**:39
Dunes, Battle of the **7**:27
Dunhuang **2**:39
Dupleix, Joseph **8**:23, 26
Durand Line **9**:45
Dürer, Albrecht **6**:20
Dustbowl **10**:20, 49
Dutch Republic **7**:23, 26, 34, 36–37
Dutch traders **6**:43, **7**:11, 12, 14, 31, *36*

Easter Island **2**:35, **3**:*42*, *43*, **8**:14, 47
Eastern Woodlands people **3**:32
Easter Rising **10**:12, 49
East India Company
   British **8**:11, 29, 31, 32, 33, 35, 47, **9**:18,
      24, 49
   Danish **8**:15, 47
   Dutch **7**:11, 36, 39, 47, **8**:6, 43, 48
   English **6**:8, **7**:11, 14, 18, 22, 31, 38, 39,
      47, **8**:23, *32*
   French **7**:34, 47, **8**:23, 48
   United (VOC) **8**:33
East India trade **8**:32–33
East Timor **10**:27, 39, 47, 49
Ebola virus **10**:46
Ecuador **9**:16
Eddystone Lighthouse **8**:27
Edessa, Treaty of **3**:12
Edington, Battle of **3**:37, 39
Edirne **5**:22, 33
Edison, Thomas Alva **9**:23, *36*, 37, 39, **10**:18
Edo **7**:7, 34, **8**:6, 39
Edward of England **5**:10
Edward I of England **5**:18
Edward II of England **5**:18, 19
Edward IV of England **5**:38
Edward VI of England **6**:40–41
Edward VII of Great Britain **10**:6
Edward the Black Prince **5**:22, 23, 26
Edward the Confessor **4**:12, 13, 14
Egypt **1**:25, 38, 39, **2**:7, 39, **3**:17, 24, 33,
      9:38, **10**:25
   Alexander the Great and **2**:10, 11
   autonomy from Turkey **9**:18
   British occupation **9**:40, 41, 42, **10**:12
   dynasties **1**:10, 11, *14*, 16, 19, 30
   First Intermediate Kingdom **1**:15, 16
   Greek Ptolemies **1**:25, **2**:10, *13*, 18, 32
   Middle Kingdom **1**:50
   New Kingdom **1**:19, 23, 24–25
   Old Kingdom **1**:*11*, 16–17
   Second Intermediate Period **1**:52
Eichmann, Adolf **10**:29, 32
Eiffel Tower **9**:43
Einstein, Albert **10**:21
Eisenhower, Dwight D. **10**:28
Elam **1**:22

Elamites **1**:47
El Cid **4**:11, *18*, 19, 48
Eleanor of Aquitaine **4**:27, 28, 29, 30
electricity **9**:36
electrons, discovery **9**:47
elevators **9**:*26*, 27
Elijah **1**:31
Elisha **1**:31
Elizabeth I of England **6**:25, 26, 27, 39,
      40–41, 42
Elizabeth Petrovna **8**:22
Ellora **3**:*28*
El Mirador **2**:7, 15, 18, 23, 27, 31, 48
El Paso **7**:27
emaki **4**:26, *27*
Emancipation Proclamation **9**:30
Empire State Building **10**:17
Encyclopedia **8**:16, *17*, 23, 35, 48
encyclopedias, in China **3**:33, 44
Engels, Friedrich **9**:24
engines **7**:43, **9**:6, 23, 37, **10**:10
English civil war **7**:28–29
Enlightenment **8**:16–17, *27*, 35, 48
Entente Cordiale **10**:6, 49
Enver Pasha **10**:9
Epic of Gilgamesh **1**:10, 19
Equiano, Olaudah **8**:39
Erasmus **6**:20, *21*
Eratosthenes **2**:15, 48
Erie Canal **9**:14
Erik Bloodaxe **3**:39, 44
Erik the Red **3**:39, 45
Erik "the Saint" **4**:27
Eritrea **10**:25
Esarhaddon **1**:38
Escorial **6**:30, *31*
Esfahan **6**:43, **7**:8, 9, 34, **8**:11, 15, 38, **10**:7
Esmail I of Persia **6**:6, 10, 15, **7**:8
Estates-General **5**:14, 47, **7**:10, 47, **8**:39,
      45, 48
Estonia **6**:30, **8**:8, 15
Estrada Cabrera, Manuel **10**:12
Ethiopia **5**:35, 38, **7**:23, *42*, 43, **9**:42, 43,
      43, 46, **10**:12, 15, 20, 39, 40
Etruscans **1**:34, 38, **2**:40–41, 48, **2**:6, 7, 25, 48
Euclid **2**:14, 48
European Community **10**:41
European Economic Community **10**:*28*, 35
European Union **10**:25, 28, 45, 47, 49
Everest, Mt. **10**:28
Evesham, Battle of **5**:7
exploration
   Age of Discovery **5**:44–45
   Russia's drive to the east **7**:40–41
   in the wake of Columbus **6**:8–9
Exxon Valdez **10**:44

Factory Act **9**:22
Faeroe Islands **3**:29, 39
Fa-hsien **2**:39
Faisal I of Iraq **10**:17
Falklands War **10**:40
"False Messiah" **7**:30, *31*, 48
Family Compact **8**:29, 48
Fa Ngum **5**:22
Fante Confederation **9**:34, 49
Fan Zhongyan **4**:8
Faraday, Michael **9**:36, *37*
Farrukhsiyar **8**:11
Fashoda Incident **9**:47
Fath Ali Shah **8**:43, **9**:6
Fatimids **3**:23, *40*, 41, 44, 49, **4**:14, 18, 19, 48
Fawkes, Guido (Guy) **7**:6
Fehrbellin, Battle of **7**:35
Fenians **9**:27, 49
Ferdinand III, *Holy Roman emp.* **7**:19
Ferdinand II of Aragon **5**:43, **6**:6
Ferdinand II of Bohemia **7**:16
Ferdinand III of Castile **4**:43

Ferdinand VII of Spain **9**:12, 14
Fermi, Enrico **10**:22
Fernando III **4**:42
feudalism **3**:49, **4**:28–29
Fez **3**:32, 36, **9**:49
Fiji **10**:27, 35, 41
Firdausi **3**:41, **4**:6, 7
Firuz Shah **5**:22, 26
Firuz Shah Bahmani **5**:30, 31
fission, nuclear **10**:21
flagellants **5**:*20*
flight **9**:23, **10**:*8*, 10
Flinders, Matthew **9**:6
Florence **5**:11, 31, 42, **6**:20
Florida **8**:20, 35, **9**:13
flying machines **6**:6
food, genetically modified **10**:45
Forbidden City **5**:31, 48, **7**:48
Ford, Henry, and Ford cars **10**:10–*11*
Foreign Legion **9**:28
Fort Orange **7**:12
Fort Ross **9**:8
Fourteenth Amendment **9**:34
Fourth of May Movement **10**:13, 49
Fox Talbot, William Henry **9**:*20*
Francis I of France **6**:15, 18, 20, *21*, 23
Francis II Rakoczi **8**:6
Francis of Assissi, St. **4**:*38*, 39, 42
Francis Joseph (Franz Josef) I **9**:25, 31
Franco, Francisco **10**:21, 38
Franco-Prussian War **9**:*34*, 35, 49
Frankfurt, Treaty of **9**:35
Frankish Kingdom **2**:44, **3**:10–11, 28, 38, 49
Franklin, Benjamin **8**:*18*, 26, 27, 42
Franz Ferdinand **10**:12
Frederick I Barbarossa **4**:29, 30, 34, 35, 43, 45
Frederick II, *Holy Roman emp.* **4**:20, 39,
      42, 43, *44*–45
Frederick I of Prussia **8**:6, 23, 25
Frederick II (the Great) of Prussia **8**:16, *17*,
      24, *25*, 26, 28, 29, 39
Frederick William of Brandenburg **8**:24, 25
Frederick William I of Prussia **8**:18, 22, 24, 25
Frederick William II of Prussia **8**:25
Frederick William III of Prussia **8**:25, **9**:20
Frederick William IV of Prussia **9**:20, 24
Freedom Riders **10**:32, 49
Free Soilers **9**:26
Fremont Culture **4**:11
French and Indian War **7**:48, **8**:27, *28*, 29, 48
French Revolution **8**:*38*, 42, 44–45
Frobisher, Martin **6**:35
Froissart, Jean **5**:30
Fuad I of Egypt **10**:14
Fugitive Slave Act **9**:25
Fuji, mt. **8**:7
Fujiwara clan **3**:36, 50, **4**:30, 48
Fujiwara Michinaga **3**:45
Funan **2**:39, 48, **3**:12, 50
Funj **6**:6, 48, **8**:30, 48
Fyodor III of Russia **7**:35, **8**:8

Gadhafi, Muammar al- **10**:34, 40
Gadsden Purchase **9**:26, 49
Gagarin, Yuri **10**:32, *36*
Galatia **2**:14, 15, 48
Galileo Galilei **7**:*11*, 18, 44
Gallipoli **10**:12
Gallipoli Peninsula **5**:33
Gama, Vasco da **5**:43, 44, *45*
Gambia **8**:15, **9**:21
Gandhi, Indira **10**:33, 38, 40
Gandhi, "Mahatma" **10**:12, 14, 16, 17, 20,
      21, 23, 25
Gandhi, Rajiv **10**:45
Ganges Valley **1**:30
Gang of Four **10**:39
Gao **4**:30, **5**:16, 18, 26
Gao, *Dowager Empress* **4**:8, 9, 18

Gaozong **4**:9
Gao Zong **4**:26, 27
Garasanin, Ilija **9**:21
Garfield, James **9**:40
Garibaldi, Giuseppe **9**:27, 31
Garnier, François **9**:35
Gaugamela, Battle of **2**:12
Gaugin, Paul **9**:44, *45*
Gaul **2**:25, 44, 48, 2:48
Gaulle, Charles de **10**:22, 32
Gauls **1**:40, **2**:7, 10
Gempei War **4**:34
Genghis Khan **4**:31, 36, 38, 39, *40, 41*, 42, 48, **5**:12, 13, 48, **8**:48
Geoffrey of Monmouth **4**:29
George I of Great Britain **8**:11
George II of Great Britain **8**:18, 23, 29, 30
George III of Great Britain **8**:29, 30, **9**:9
George V of Great Britain **10**:8, *9*
Georgia (America) **8**:19, 20, 22
Georgia (Caucasus) **4**:34, 38, **5**:48, **7**:11, 48, **9**:49
Gerbert of Aurillac **3**:41, 45
Germany **2**:26, **9**:26, **10**:15
  East and West **10**:24, 44
Geronimo **9**:41
Ghana **10**:28
Ghana, Kingdom of **3**:45, 50, **4**:18, 34, 48, **5**:48
Ghazali, al- **4**:14, 23
Ghazan, Mahmud **5**:11, 15
Ghaznavid Dynasty **3**:44, 50, **4**:10, *16*, 36, 48
Ghazni **4**:30, 31
Ghiasuddin Balban **5**:7
Ghiasuddin Tughluq **5**:15
Ghibellines **4**:*43*, **5**:6, 48
Ghiberti, Lorenzo **5**:30
Ghilzai Afghans **8**:11, 48
Ghuri, Muhammad **4**:31, 34, 36, 37, 38
Ghurid Dynasty **4**:22, 35, 36, 48
Gibraltar **8**:15, 48
Gilbert, Sir Humphrey **6**:38
Gilbert, William **7**:44
Gilgamesh **1**:10, 12, 48
gins, cotton **8**:*43*
Giotto **5**:18
Gladstone, William **9**:41, 43
glassmaking **2**:22
Glenn, John **10**:36
Globe Theater **6**:41
Goa **6**:10, 48, **7**:48, **10**:32
Goband Singh **7**:34
Go-Daigo **5**:*15*, 19
Godunov, Boris **6**:39, *43*
Golden Horde **4**:41, 43, 48, **5**:6, 27, 28, 34, 42, 48, **6**:6, 48
gold rushes **9**:*24*, 25, *40*, 47
Gondar **7**:*42*
Good Friday Agreement **10**:46
Good Hope, Cape of **5**:42, 43, 44
Gorbachev, Mikhail **10**:30, *31, 40*
Gordon, Charles **9**:40, *41*
Gothic churches **4**:*26*, 48
Goths **2**:34
Government of India Act **8**:33, **9**:27, **10**:20
Goya, Francisco de **9**:9
Gracchus, Tiberius **2**:19, 53
Granada **5**:18, 48
Granada, Treaty of **6**:6, 53
Grand Canal, China **2**:27, **3**:16, **5**:*18*, 19, 31
Granicus, Battle of **2**:12
Great Depression **10**:16, *17*, 50
Great Enclosure **4**:38, *39*
Greater Chiriqui **2**:19
Great Exhibition, London **9**:25
Great Fire of London **7**:30
Great Flood **1**:10, 12
Great Northern War **8**:6, 7, 8, *10*, 15, 48
Great Pharmacopoeia **6**:35

Great Pyramid at Giza **1**:11, 17, 48
Great Schism **5**:26, 31, 48
Great Stupa **2**:23
Great Wall of China **2**:11, *16*, 17, 18, 48, **5**:*39*, 48, **10**:*35*
Great Zimbabwe **4**:34, 49, **5**:30, *35*, 48, **6**:*12–13*, **7**:48
Greco, El **6**:35
Greece **1**:23, 35, **2**:6, 8–9, **4**:23, **9**:12, 13, 15, **10**:24
  city-states **2**:8–9
  Homer's **1**:32–33
Greenland, Vikings **3**:39, 45
Gregory VII, *Pope* **4**:15, 17, 19, 44, *45*
Gregory 13, *Pope* **6**:31
Grenada **10**:40
Grosseilliers, Médard Chouart des **7**:27, 31
Guadalupe, Virgin of **7**:23, 53
Guadeloupe **7**:18
Guam **7**:31
Guatemala **1**:31, **6**:15, **9**:20
Guatemala City **8**:34, **10**:12
Guelphs **4**:*43*, **5**:6, 48
Guericke, Otto von **7**:44
Guevara, Che **10**:33
Guido D'Arrezzo **4**:10
Guillaume de Loris **4**:42
guillotines **8**:*45*
Gujarat **4**:26, **6**:48, **7**:48
Gulf War **10**:44, *45*, 50
Gulliver's Travels **8**:*15*
Gulnabad, Battle of **8**:14
Gunbad-i Qabus **4**:6
gunpowder **3**:36, **4**:11, 27
Gunpowder Plot **7**:6, 7
gunpowder revolution **6**:44–45
Gupta Empire **2**:*37*, 39, 42, 48, **3**:50
Gupta period **3**:8
Gurkhas **8**:31, 48, **9**:9, 12, 49
Gustavus I of Sweden **6**:15
Gustavus II Adolphus **7**:10, 14, *16*, 18
Gutenberg, Johannes **5**:38, *40*, 41, 48
Haakon VII of Norway **10**:7
hacienda system **8**:20, 48
Hadrian **2**:29, 30, *31*, 48
Hadrian's Wall **2**:29, 31, 48
Hafiz **5**:23
Haidar Ali **8**:*30*, 31, 34, 35, 38
Haile Selassie I **10**:16, 20, 35
Hairun of Ternate **6**:31
Haiti **8**:13, 42, **9**:7
Halicarnassus, Mausoleum at **2**:10
Halifax, Nova Scotia **8**:23
Hallstatt Culture **1**:27, 31, 48
Hamadi Dynasty **8**:30
Hammadids **4**:6, 49
Hammarskjöld, Dag **10**:32
Hammurabi **1**:*18*, 48
Handel, George Frederick **8**:22
Han Dynasty **2**:19, 26, 31, 48
Hannibal **2**:15, 24, 25, 48
Hanno **2**:7
Hanoi **9**:35
Hanoverian Dynasty **8**:11, 49
Hanseatic League **4**:43, 49, **5**:23, 48
Hanzhou **5**:12
Hapsburg Dynasty **5**:35, 42, 48, **6**:48, **7**:7, 32, 43, 48, **8**:*22*, 49
Hara Castle, massacre at **7**:21
Harald Bluetooth **3**:39
Harappa **1**:14, 18, 20, 48
Hardings, Lord **10**:8
Harding, Warren **10**:14, 15
Harihara II **5**:30
Harington, John **6**:42
Harold II **4**:12–13, 14
harquebuses **6**:*45*, 48
Harrison, John **8**:18
Harshavardhana **3**:16, 17, 20

Hartog, Dirk **8**:40
Harun al-Rashid **3**:23, 29, 32
Harvard University **7**:19
Harvey, William **7**:15, 44
Hasan Pasha **8**:6
Haskalah **8**:16, 49
Hasmonean Dynasty **2**:32, 33
Hassan II of Morocco **10**:38
Hastings, Battle of **4**:12–13, 14
Hastings, Warren **8**:32, 33, 35, 38
Hatshepsut **1**:22, 24, 48
Hattin, Battle of **4**:20, 31, 34
Hausa states **4**:35, 49, **5**:48, **6**:48, **7**:10, **9**:6, 49, **10**:50
Hawaii **9**:13, 45, 47
Hawaiian Islands **2**:42, **3**:42–43
Hawke, Bob **10**:40
Hayam Wuruk **5**:23
Hazen, al- **3**:44, **4**:10
Heidelberg, University of **5**:26
Hein, Piet **7**:15
Hellenistic Period **2**:32, 48
Hemchandra **4**:26
Henchak **9**:40, 49
Henry III, *Holy Roman emp.* **4**:11
Henry IV, *Holy Roman emp.* **4**:15, 19, 44, 45
Henry I of England **4**:22, 26
Henry II of England, (Henry of Anjou) **4**:28, 29, 30, 31
Henry III of England **5**:6, 7
Henry IV of England **5**:27
Henry V of England **5**:31
Henry VI of England **5**:38
Henry VIII of England **6**:7, 18, 19, 24, 25, 40
Henry II of France **6**:23
Henry III of France **6**:35
Henry IV of France **6**:39, 42, **7**:10
Henry V of Germany **4**:23
Henry the Navigator **5**:31, 35, *44*
Heraclius **3**:7, 16, 17
Herat **5**:39, **9**:26
Herculaneum **2**:27
Hero of Alexandria **2**:27, 48
Herod the Great **2**:22, 23, 32, 48
Herodotus **1**:39, **2**:7, 49
Herschel, William **8**:38
Herzl, Theodor **9**:47, **10**:6
Hesiod **1**:32, 35, 48
Hidalgo, Michael **9**:8
Hidetada **7**:15
Hideyori **7**:10
Hideyoshi **6**:35, *38*, 39, 42, 43, **7**:20
hijra (Hejira) **3**:16, 18, 50
Himiko **2**:34
Hinduism **2**:39, 42, 49, **4**:*23*, **6**:48, **7**:48
Hipparchus **2**:19, 49
Hippo **2**:43
Hippocrates **2**:6, 49
Hiram I **1**:27
Hirohito **10**:15, 44
Hiroshima **10**:23
Hispania **2**:18
Hispaniola **6**:48, **9**:13, 21
Hitler, Adolf **10**:*20*
Hittites **1**:19, 22, *23*, 48
Ho Chi Minh **10**:13
Hofer, Andreas **9**:8
Hohenstaufen family **4**:43, 44, 49, **5**:48
Hohokam Culture **2**:14, 38, 49, **4**:*6*, 26, *32, 33*, 35, 48, **5**:6, 31
Hojo family **4**:39, 49
Hokusai **9**:*14*
Hollywood **10**:*19*, 25
Holy Land **4**:21, **5**:*9*
Holy League **6**:10, 48, **7**:39, 48
Holy Roman Empire **3**:*44*, **4**:44–45, **5**:48, 7:48, **9**:7, 50
Holy Sepulchre Church **4**:7, *21*

Homer **1**:32, 33, 48
hominids **1**:6, 48
Homs, Battle of **5**:8, 10
Hong Kong **9**:20, 21, 28, **10**:*46*, 47
Hongwu **5**:27
Hoover, Herbert **10**:16
Hoover Dam **10**:20, *21*
Hopewell Culture **2**:22, 39, 49, **3**:17, **4**:32, 49
Hormuz **7**:14, 48
Horn, Cape **7**:11
horoscope, earliest **2**:7
horse collars **4**:22
horses **1**:8, *9*, 19, 26
Horthy, Nikolaus **10**:14
Hospitalers **4**:20
Houtman, Cornelis **6**:42, *43*
Huang Di **1**:11, 48
Huan of Qi **1**:44
Huari Empire **2**:43, **3**:12, *13*, 24, 32
Huayna Capac **5**:37, **6**:6
Hubble Space Telescope **10**:37, *45*
Hubertsburg, Peace of **8**:31
Hudson, Henry **7**:7, *10*
Huerta, Victoriano **10**:9
Hugh Capet **3**:45
Hugo, Victor **9**:30
Huguenots **6**:25, 27, 30, 34, 49, **7**:15, 32, 33, 39, 48, **8**:25, 49
Huitziláhuitl **5**:26
Human Genome Project **10**:44, 50
humans, early **1**:6–7
Humayun **6**:*18*, 22, 26, *36*, 37
Humboldt, Alexander von **9**:6
Hundred Years' War **5**:18, 22, 30, 38, 49
Hungary **6**:22, **7**:7, 43, **8**:6, **10**:14, 28
Huns **2**:38, 39, 42, 43, *45*, 49, **3**:50
Hus, Jan **5**:*31*
Husain Baiqara **5**:39
Husain ibn Ali **8**:6
Husainid Dynasty **8**:7, 49
Husayn (grandson of Muhammad) **3**:22, *23*
Husayn, Mirza **9**:35
Husein, Sharif **10**:13
Hussein, Saddam **10**:47
Hussein of Jordan **10**:34, 46
Hussein of Persia **7**:42
Hussites **5**:35, 49
Hussite Wars **6**:44, 49
Huygens, Christiaan **7**:36, 45
Hyderabad **6**:42, **8**:10, 15, 49
Hyderabad, Battle of **9**:21
Hyksos **1**:18, 24–25
Hypatia **2**:42

Ibn Abd al-Hakam **3**:36
Ibn Battuta **5**:15, 16, 18, 22, 26
Ibn Khaldun **5**:19, 23, 27
Ibn Tumert **4**:22, 26
Ibrahim the Mad **7**:22, 23
Ibrahim Pasha **9**:24
Iceland **3**:29, 36, 41
Iceni tribe **2**:27
Iconoclast Controversy **3**:50
Idris III Aloma **6**:34, 38
Idrisid Dynasty **3**:29
Ieharu **8**:30, 38
Iemitsu **7**:15, 19, 21, 26
Ienobu **8**:7
Ieyoshi **9**:19
Ifriqiya **4**:42, 49
Igbo Culture **3**:*41*, 50
Igor Svyatoslavich **4**:34
Ilkhan Dynasty **5**:19, 49
Ilkhanids **5**:10, 11, 15
Illuminati, Order of **8**:17, 49
Impressionism **9**:*38*
incanabula **5**:*41*
Incas **4**:27, 38, 49, **5**:34, *36–37*, 39, 42, 49, **6**:6, 16, *17*, 49, **8**:49

Independence, Declaration of **8**:35, 36, 47
Independence, Dutch War of **6**:34
India **1**:23, 30, **9**:30, 46, **10**:12, 16, 20
    arrival of Islam **4**:35, **36–37**
    empires **2**:36–37
    partition **10**:24, *27*
Indian Councils Act **10**:8
Indian Mutiny **8**:33, **9**:27, 28, *29*
Indian National Congress **9**:41, 50
Indian Removal Act **9**:15
Indies, Laws of the **6**:22, 50
Indo-Aryan Culture **1**:23
Indochina **9**:27, 28, **10**:26, 27, 50
Indonesia **10**:16, 24, 26
Indravarman I **3**:37
Industrial Revolution **9**:22–23
Indus Valley civilization **1**:14, 19, **20–21**, 49
Innocent III, *Pope* **4**:20, 21, 35, 39
Innocent, IV, *Pope* **4**:43, **5**:6
Inquisition **4**:43, 49, **5**:49, **6**:49, **7**:18, 48
    Spanish **5**:42, **6**:31
International Peace Conference, First **9**:47
Internet **10**:19
invention, age of **9**:36–37
Investiture Contest **4**:15, 44, *45*, 49
Ionia **1**:31, 32, **2**:6, 8, 49
Ipsos, Battle of **2**:13
Iramavataram **4**:27
Iran **4**:14, **8**:6, 11, **10**:6, 8, 28
Iranian Revolution **10**:*39*
Iran–Iraq War **10**:39, 50
Iraq **10**:28, 39, 47
Ireland **9**:*21*, 24, 43, **10**:9
    Northern **10**:14, 34, 46
    Vikings **3**:32, 33, 38, **4**:6
Irene, *Empress* **3**:*28*, 29
Irfan **8**:11
iron **1**:18, 23, 26, 31, 32, 38, 39, 44, **2**:6, 7,
    10, 15, 31, **4**:8, **8**:19, 26
Iron Age **3**:8, 45
Iron Bridge **8**:*35*
Iroquois **4**:*19*, **5**:23, 49, **7**:49, **8**:49
Irwin Declaration **10**:16
Isabella II of Spain **9**:21
Isabella of Castile **5**:39, 43, **6**:6
Isabella of England **5**:18
Isayu I of Ethiopia **7**:38, 42
Ishmail Pasha **9**:13
Islam **6**:48
    comes to India **4**:35, **36–37**
    Muhammad and **3**:12, 16, **18–19**, 23, **7**:49
    Sunnis and Shiites **3**:22–23
Islam Shah **6**:23
Ismail, Mulay **7**:34
Ismail of Egypt **9**:30
Israel **10**:*24*, 25, 34, 45
Israel, kingdom of **1**:27, **28–29**
Israelites, Exodus **1**:23, 47
Issus River, Battle of the **2**:12, 49
Istanbul (Constantinople) **2**:42, *43*, **3**:*6*, 9,
    20, **4**:39, **5**:7, *32–33*, 38, **6**:7
    mosques **6**:*19*, 27, *29*, **7**:*7*
    Varangians and **3**:7, 36, 46–47
Italy **6**:*21*, **10**:24
Iturbide, Agustín **9**:16
Ivan I of Moscow **5**:18
Ivan III of Moscow **5**:39, 49, **6**:6
Ivan the Terrible (Ivan IV) **6**:23, 31, **32–33**, **7**:40
Ivory Coast **9**:42, 43, **10**:18
Izapa **2**:14, 49

Jabir al-Sabab **9**:8
Jabir ibn Aflah **4**:27
Jabir ibn Hayyan **3**:29
Jacobites **8**:11, 49
Jacquard, Joseph **9**:22, **10**:42
Jaffna **5**:10
Jagannath Temple **4**:22, *23*
Jagiellon Dynasty **5**:30, 49

Jahangir **6**:36–37, **7**:6, 7, 11, 15
Jahan Shah **5**:34, 39
Jainism **4**:26, 49, **6**:49
Jalaluddin Rumi **5**:7
Jamaica **7**:27, 34, **8**:43, **9**:19, **10**:*26*, 27
Jamal al-Din al-Afghani **9**:45, 46
James Edward Stuart **8**:11
James I of Aragon **5**:6
James I of England (James VI of Scotland)
    6:41, **7**:6, 15
James II of Great Britain **7**:39, 42
Jameson Raid **9**:46
Jamestown **7**:6, 11, 12, 13, 23, 49
Janissaries **5**:32, *33*, 49, **6**:38, 49, **7**:14, *15*,
    27, 49, **8**:18, 49, **9**:*7*, 14, 50
Jansz, Willem **8**:40
Japan **3**:17, **9**:30
    Buddhism **3**:21, *26*, *27*, 33, **4**:39
    closed to foreigners **7**:20–21
    rise of **3**:26–27
Java **3**:32, **5**:11, **7**:15, 23, 36, 39, **8**:32, **9**:8, 9, 15
Javanese Wars of Succession **8**:6, 11, 49
Jaya Sthiti **5**:26
Jayavarman I **3**:20
Jayavarman II **3**:33, **4**:34
Jayavarman VII **4**:25
Jayavarman VIII **5**:11
Jazz Singer, The **10**:*16*, 18
Jefferson, Thomas **9**:6
Jenkins' Ear, War of **8**:20, 53
Jenné-Jeno **2**:42, **5**:49
Jenner, Edward **8**:43
Jerusalem **1**:26, 29, 35, 42, **2**:7, **3**:16
    crusaders and **4**:19, 20, 29, 31, 42
    taken by Saladin **4**:31, 34
    Temple **1**:27, 28, *29*, 43, **2**:22, 33
Jesuits **6**:22, 23, 39, 49, **7**:31, 49, **8**:11, 20,
    27, 30, 31, 34, 49
Jesus Christ **2**:23, 26, 40
Jews **1**:22, **5**:20, 38, **8**:16, **9**:40, 47, **10**:*22*
    Diaspora **1**:29, **2**:*32–33*
Jezebel **1**:31
Jimmu **1**:38, 49
Jin **2**:6
Jin Dynasty and Empire **4**:*9*, *22*, 23, 26, 38,
    39, 40, 43, 49, **5**:12, 49
Jinnah, Muhammad Ali **10**:*21*
Joan of Arc **5**:*34*
John, *king of England* **4**:29, 39
John III Sobieski **7**:35, *38*
John III Vatatzes **4**:38
John IV of Portugal **9**:8, 15
John Paul II, *Pope* **10**:*39*, 47
Johnson, Andrew **9**:34
Johnson, Lyndon B. **10**:32
Johnson, Samuel **8**:16
John Tzimisces **3**:46
Joinville, Jean de **5**:15
Joliet, Louis **7**:34
Jones, Jim **10**:38
Jordan **10**:24, 25, 45
Joseph I, *Holy Roman emp.* **8**:6
Joseph II, *Holy Roman emp.* **8**:38
Juan Carlos **10**:38
Juan-Juan **2**:42, 49, **3**:12, 50
Juárez, Benito **9**:35
Judah **1**:27, 28, 29, 42, 49
Judea **2**:22, *26*, 33
Jugurtha **2**:19
Julian **2**:39
Julius II, *Pope* **6**:6, 7, 20
July Revolution **9**:15, 50
Jürchen people **4**:22, 23, 49, **5**:49
Justinian I **3**:*6*, 9
Juvenal **2**:31, 49

Kaaba, the **3**:*18*, **6**:*11*, 49
Kabir **5**:34
Kabir, Ali Bey al- **8**:31

Kabul **8**:34, **9**:20
Kabul Khan **4**:40
Kachina Cult **5**:18, 49
Kadesh, Battle of **1**:22, 24, 49
Kahina "the Prophetess" **3**:24
Kaifeng **4**:30, 43, 49
Kairouan **3**:21
Kalka River, Battle of **4**:40
Kamakura Period **4**:34, *35*, 50, **5**:11, 15, 19, 49
Kamchatka Peninsula **7**:*40*
Kamehameha I **9**:*8*
Kammu **3**:26, 27, 29
Kandahar **6**:42, **7**:14, 15, 18, **8**:7
Kandarya Mahadeva Temple **4**:11
Kandy, Kingdom of **6**:22, 49, **7**:26, 49, **8**:30, 49
Kanem, Kingdom of **3**:32, **4**:39, 50, **6**:49
Kanem-Bornu **4**:19, **6**:34
Kang De **10**:20
Kangxi **7**:24, 25, **8**:14
Kanishka **2**:30, 49
Kansas–Nebraska Act **9**:26
Kante Dynasty **4**:34, 50
Kappel, Battle of **6**:18
Kara George **9**:6, 9
Kara-Khitai **4**:40
Karakorum **4**:42
Kara Koyunlu (Black Sheep) **5**:26
Karanaga people **6**:12, 13
Karbala **3**:20, 22, *23*, **7**:9
Karelia **7**:*7*, 49
Karim Khan Zand **8**:35
Karkar, Battle of **1**:28, 31
Karlowitz, Treaty of **7**:43, **8**:10
Kartarpur **6**:11
Karthoum **9**:40
Kashgaria **8**:27, 49
Kashmir **9**:12, **10**:25, 32
Kashta **1**:34, 49
Kasr al-Kabir **6**:35
Kaunda, Kenneth **10**:44
Kay, John **8**:*18*, **9**:22
Kazembe IV **9**:21, 50
Kemmu Restoration **5**:19, 49
Kennedy, John F. **10**:*32*, 36
Kennedy, Robert **10**:34
Kepler, Johannes **7**:7, 44
Khajuraho, temples **3**:32
Khalil **5**:8, 9, 10
Khalji Dynasty **4**:36, 37, 50, **5**:11
Khalsa Brotherhood **7**:43, 49
Khartoum **9**:14, 41, 42
Khatami, Mohammed **10**:46
Khazan **6**:26
Khazars **3**:16, 44, 50
Khephren **1**:*14*, 49
Khitans **3**:40, 41, 51, **4**:7, 9, 50
Khizr Khan **5**:30
Khmer Empire **3**:20, 33, 51, **4**:23, 24, 25,
    30, 34, 50, **5**:26, 34
Khmer Rouge **10**:*38*, 39, 50
Khomeini, Ayatollah **10**:32, 38, *39*, 44
Khorasan (Khurasan) **3**:24, **4**:35, 50, **6**:10,
    26, 43, 49, **7**:9
Khosrow I **3**:9, 13
Khosrow II **3**:13, 16
Khwarazm, Kingdom of **4**:40, 41, 50
Khwarazmi **4**:43
Khwarazmian Turks **4**:30, 35, 42
Khwarizmi, Al- **3**:32
Kiev **3**:36, 39, 46, **4**:11, 41, 50
Kilwa **4**:50 **5**:18, **6**:6, 49
King, Martin Luther **10**:32, *33*, 34
King George's War **8**:22, 49
King Philip's War **7**:34, *35*
King Sejong **5**:35

King William's War **7**:38, 42, 43, 49
Kirina, Battle of **5**:16
Kitchener, Herbert **9**:47
Kizimkazi, Friday Mosque **4**:22
knights **4**:*20*
Knights Templar **5**:15, 49
Knossos **1**:*33*, 49
Kobad **2**:43
Kobé earthquake **10**:46
Koguryo **2**:38, 49, **3**:51
Kojiki **3**:24
Kokand **8**:27, 49, **9**:38, 50
Kokom Dynasty **5**:10
Kolin, Battle of **8**:26, 29
Kongo, Kingdom of **5**:27, 49, **6**:13, 14, 23,
    26, 30, 34, 49, **7**:30, 31, 49, **8**:7
Konjaku monogatari **4**:23
Köprülü family **7**:30, 39, 42
Koran **3**:*19*, 20, 40, 51, **4**:27, 50
Korea **1**:15, **2**:39, 42, **4**:31, 41, 42, **5**:6, 26,
    6:7, 42, 43, **7**:15, **8**:38, **9**:6, 34, 39, 40,
    46, **10**:7, 8
    North and South **10**:24, 47
Korean War **10**:24, 28, 50
Koryo **3**:41, 51, **4**:23, 50
Kosovo **10**:46, 47, 50
Kosovo, Battles of **5**:33
Kotte **6**:10, 22, 26, 50
Kowloon **9**:47
Krak des Chevaliers **4**:*21*
Krakow, University of **5**:22
Kremlin **5**:23
Krishnadevaraya **6**:7
Krishnaraja I **3**:29
Kublai Khan **4**:9, 24, 25, 41, **5**:6, 7, 10, 11,
    12, 13, 49
Kuchuk-Kainarji, Treaty of **8**:35
Kulottunga I of Vengi **4**:15
Kumarapala **4**:26
Kunnersdorf, Battle of **8**:27, 29
Kuomintang **9**:46, 50, **10**:9, 14, 21, 24
Kurds **9**:39, 50, **10**:15, 41, 50
Kush **1**:30, 39, 49
Kushans **2**:26, 27, 30, 34, 35, 36, 37, 49
Kushites **1**:38
Kuwait **10**:32, 44
Kyakhta, Treaty of **8**:14
Kyoto **4**:14, 15, **5**:38

Lalibela **4**:30, 38
Lambart, Thomas **7**:14
lamps (lights), electric **9**:23, 36
Langland, William **5**:22
Lan Na **6**:27
Lannatai **5**:7, 50
Lansdowne, Lord **9**:44
Lan Xang **5**:42, 50, **8**:7, 10, 50
Lao people **5**:22
Laos **6**:50, **7**:49, **8**:6, 10, **9**:15, 35, 44
Laozu **4**:*8*
Lapita Culture **1**:49 **2**:15, 49
Lapita people **1**:23, 26
La Rochelle **5**:23, **7**:15
Lars Porsena **1**:43
La Salle, René-Robert Cavelier, sieur de
    7:31, 38
las Casa, Bartolomé de **6**:*23*, 26
Las Navas de Tolosa, Battle of **4**:39
La Tène culture **2**:6, 7, 49
Latin America, liberation of **9**:16–17
Latins and Latin kingdoms **4**:22, 23, 50, **5**:9, 50
League of Augsburg, War of the **7**:32, 39, 53
League of Nations **10**:13, 14, 20, 50
Lebanon **10**:14, 22, 38, 40
Lebna Denegel **6**:6, 22
Lechfeld, Battle of **3**:44
Lee, Robert E. **9**:31, 33
Leeuwenhoek, Antoni van **7**:*44*, 45
Legnano, Battle of **4**:34, 43, 45

Leif Eriksson **3**:*45*
Lenin, Vladimir **10**:*13*, 15
Leo III, *Pope* **3**:6, 7
Leo X, *Pope* **6**:*24*
Leo III, *Emperor* **3**:6, 24
Leon Africanus **5**:42
Leonardo da Vinci **5**:39, 43, **6**:6, *20*
Leonardo Fibonacci **4**:38
Leopold I, *Holy Roman emp.* **8**:6, 7, 27
Leopold I of Belgium **9**:18
Leopold II of Belgium **9**:40, 42–43
Lepanto, Battle of **6**:34, *35*
leprosy **4**:42
Lesseps, Ferdinand de **9**:39
Lessing, Gotthold Ephraim **8**:*16*
Lewis and Clark expedition **9**:7
Lexington, Battle of **8**:34
Liang Dynasty **3**:8, 51
Liao **4**:23, 50
Liao Dynasty **3**:41
Liberia **9**:24, 30, *43*
Liberty, Statue of **9**:*41*
Library of Congress, U.S. **9**:6
Libya **10**:27
Liegnitz, Battle of **4**:41
Lima **6**:17, 19, 22, **8**:23
Lincoln, Abraham **9**:27, 30, 31, 32, *33*
Lindbergh, Charles **10**:10, 16
Linné, Karl (Carolus Linnaeus) **8**:16, *19*
Lisbon **4**:20, **8**:16, 26
Lithuania **5**:26, 50, **6**:31, **10**:44
Little Big Horn, Battle of the **9**:38
Little Rock high school **10**:29
Liu Bang **2**:17, 49
Live Aid **10**:40, *41*
Livingstone, David **9**:31, 34, *35*, 42
Livonia **6**:32, 50, **7**:14, 49, **8**:8, 15
Li Yuanhao **4**:10
Llywelyn ap Gruffudd **5**:7
Locke, John **7**:39, **8**:16
Lockerbie **10**:41
locomotives **9**:*15*, *36*
Lodi Dynasty **5**:38, 50
Logstown Treaty **8**:26
Lombard League **4**:43, 45, 50
Lombards **3**:6, *13*, 25, 51, **4**:50
London **2**:26, **3**:41
London, Treaty of **9**:21, 34
Longinus **3**:13
looms **8**:*18*, **9**:22
Lorraine **9**:35, **10**:13
Los Angeles **8**:38
lost-wax method **4**:14, 51, **5**:30, 50
Lothair II **3**:11, **4**:23, 43
Louangphrabang **8**:7
Louis VI (the Fat) **4**:22
Louis VII of France **4**:20, 27
Louis IX (St. Louis) **4**:20, 42, **5**:*6*, 7, 8
Louis XII of France **5**:43, **6**:6
Louis XIII of France **7**:10, 14
Louis XIV of France (Sun King) **7**:*32–33*, 34, 35, 36, 38, 39, 43, **8**:7
Louis XV of France **8**:*10*, 11, 15, 29
Louis XVI of France **8**:35, 39, 42, 45
Louis XVIII of France **9**:9
Louisburg **8**:22, *29*, 50
Louisiana **8**:11, 20
Louisiana Purchase **9**:6, 50
Louis Philippe of France **9**:15, 24, 28
Louis the Pious **3**:32, 33
Luba, Kingdom of **7**:6, 49
Lublin, Union of **6**:31, 33, 53
"Lucy" **1**:6, 49
Lumière brothers **9**:46, **10**:18
Luna, Tristán de **6**:27
Lunda Empire **7**:34, 49
Luther, Martin **6**:11, 14, *24*, *25*
Lutheranism **6**:15, *24*, 50
Lutter, Battle of **7**:16

Lützen, Battle of **7**:16, 17, 18
Lu Yu **3**:29

Maastricht Treaty **10**:45
McAdam, John **9**:22
Macao **6**:8, *27*, 39, 50, **7**:38, 49, **9**:41
Macbeth **4**:11
Maccabees, Revolt of the **2**:18, 32, 49
Maccabeus, Judas **2**:18, *19*, 32, 33
McCarthy, Joseph **10**:25
Macchiavelli, Niccolò **6**:10
MacDonald, Ramsey **10**:15
Macedon **1**:39, 49
Macedonian Dynasty **3**:7, 36, 51
Machiavelli, Niccolo **6**:20
machine guns **9**:22
Machu Picchu **5**:*36*
McKenzie, Alexander **8**:43
McKinley, William **10**:6
Madagascar **7**:7, 10, 15, 23, 39, **9**:8
Madeira Islands **5**:44
Madero, Francisco **10**:8, 9
Madhav Rao II **8**:42
Madras **7**:26, **8**:23, 32
Madrid, Treaty of **8**:20, 26
madrigals **5**:19, 50
Magadha **1**:50, **2**:6, 49
Magdeburg, Siege of **7**:17, 18
Magellan, Ferdinand **6**:8, *9*, 11, 14
Maghrib **3**:32, 51, **4**:51, **5**:50
Magna Carta **4**:29, 39, 51
Magyars **3**:36, 40, *44*, 45, 51
Mahabalipuram **3**:*24*
Mahabharata **1**:27, 50, **6**:38, 50
Mahadji Sindhia **8**:38
Mahavira **1**:42
Mahdi, the **9**:41, 42, 50
Mahmud I **8**:18, 26
Mahmud II **9**:8, 14, 20
Mahmud of Ghazni **3**:44, **4**:6, 7, 10, 17, 36, *37*, 51
Maine, USS **9**:47
Majapahit Dynasty and Kingdom **5**:11, *23*, 50, **6**:6, 50
Makurra **3**:13, 51, **5**:23, 50
Malaya **9**:14, **10**:12, 26
Malaysia (Penang) **8**:38
Malaysia, Federation of **10**:32
Malcolm Barelegs **4**:22
Malcolm, John **9**:6
Malcolm X **10**:32
Mali, Empire of **4**:43, **5**:*15*, **16–17**, 18, 22
Malik en-Nasir, al- **5**:14
Malik Shah **4**:15, 17, 18
Malla Dynasty **5**:26
Mallet, Paul and Pierre **8**:19
Malplaquet, Battle of **8**:7
Malta **6**:28, 30
Mameluke Dynasty **4**:43, 51, **5**:6, 7, **8–9**, 10, 11, 14, 22, 26, 34, 50, **6**:7, 50, **8**:10
Mamun, al- **3**:32
Manchu (Qing) Dynasty **7**:10, 14, 15, 18, **24–25**, *35*, 42, **8**:11, 14, 27, **9**:26, **10**:9
Manchuria **4**:51, **10**:6, 7, 16, 20
Mandela, Nelson **10**:*27*, 44, 45
Manipur **9**:44
Mansur, al- **3**:23, 28
Mansuri Maristan **5**:10
Manuel I **4**:31
Manzikert, Battle of **4**:14
Maoris **3**:*32*, 50, **5**:18, **8**:50, **9**:12, 20, 21, 35, 50
Mao Zedong **10**:16, 21, 24, *25*, 29, 33, 39
Mapungubwe **4**:11
Maratha Kingdom **8**:22, 26, 30, 34, 38, 42, 50, **9**:7, 12
Marathon, Battle of **2**:6, 9, 50
March on Rome **9**:31, **10**:14
Marconi, Guglielmo **10**:18
Maria Theresa **8**:*22*, 38

Marie Antoinette **8**:34
Marie de Medicis **7**:10
Marinids **5**:6, 11, 19, 22, 50
Marquesas Islands **3**:42, 43
Marquette, Jacques **7**:34
Marrakesh **4**:15, 27
Marseille **1**:42
Marshall Plan **10**:24, 51
Martinique **7**:18
Marwan II **3**:25
Marx, Karl **9**:24, 31
Mary, Queen of Scots **6**:31, 41
Mary I of England **6**:24, 25, 26, 27, 41
Masada **2**:*27*, 33, 50
Masina **9**:13, 51
Massachusetts Bay Colony **7**:22
mass media **10**:**18–19**
Matamba, Kingdom of **7**:50, **8**:22, 50
matchlocks **6**:44, *45*, 50
mathematics **3**:9, 13, 32
Matsuo Basho **7**:*42*
Matthias I Corvinus **5**:39
Mau Mau uprising **10**:24, 51
Mauretania **2**:26, 50
Maurice, *Emperor* **3**:13
Mauritius **6**:43, **8**:14
Mauryan Empire **2**:11, 15, 18, 36, 50
Maximilian I of Mexico **9**:29, 30
Mayans **1**:22, 26, 35, 39, 43, 50, **2**:10, 15, 22, 23, 27, 31, 35, 42, 43, 51 **3**:9, 12, *25*, 28, **34–35**, **4**:42, **5**:50, **6**:*34*, 50
  decline **3**:37, 40, **4**:7, 19, **5**:30
  see also Bonampak; Chichén Itzá; Copán; Mayapán; Palenque; Tikal
Mayapán **4**:42, **5**:7, 10, 35, 38
Mayflower Compact **7**:13, 50
Mayo, Lord **9**:34, 35
Mazdak **2**:43
Mazzini, Giuseppe **9**:18
Mecca **3**:12, 19, 23, **6**:11, 34, 50, **9**:6, **10**:44
Medes **1**:31, 38, 42, 50
Medici family **5**:31, 34, 39, 40, 42, **6**:19, 20
Medina **3**:*18*, 19, **6**:34, **9**:6
Medusa **9**:12
Medway River, Battle of the **7**:30
Megalithic Culture **1**:26
Mehmed I **5**:31
Mehmed II (Mehmet II) **5**:*32–33*, 34, 38, 42
Mehmed III **6**:43
Mehmed IV **7**:38
Meji Restoration **9**:34
Melfi, Constitutions of **4**:45
Menander **2**:19, 50
Menelik II of Ethiopia **9**:43
Menes **1**:10
Mengazi **2**:15
Mengel, Gregor **9**:30
Mengzi (Mencius) **2**:10
Mentuhotep II **1**:15, 24, 50
Mercosur **10**:46, 51
Meroë **1**:42, **2**:7, 38, 50
Merovingian Dynasty **3**:10, 51
Merv **3**:20
Mesa Verde **4**:22, *23*, 32, 51
Mesopotamia **1**:8, 10, 43, 50, **3**:36, 51, **9**:9
Messenia **1**:35
Metacomet **7**:34, 35
Mexican Revolution **10**:8, 51
Mexican War **9**:25, 51
Mexico **9**:13, 28, 29, 35, 39, **10**:8, 9, 13
Miao rebellion **9**:26
Michael I, *Emperor* **3**:31
Michael I of Russia **7**:10
Michael VIII Palaeologus **5**:6, 7
Michelangelo **6**:6, 7, 20
microscopes **7**:*44*, 45
Midas **1**:34, 50
Midhat Pasha **9**:*34*
Milan, Edict of **2**:38, 50

Milosevic, Slobodan **10**:46
Mimbres pottery **4**:*14*, 15, *32*
Minamoto Yoshiie **4**:18, 51
Minden, Battle of **8**:29
Ming Dynasty **5**:13, 23, **24–25**, 35, **6**:15, 18, 42, 50, **7**:15, 18, 27, 50
Minh Manh **9**:12
Minoans **1**:11, *18*, 22, 32, *33*, 50
Minto, Lord **10**:7
miracle plays **5**:11, 50
Mir Mahmud **8**:11, 14, 15
Mir Wais Hotaki **8**:7
Mishnah **2**:33, 34
Mississippians **3**:33, 51, **4**:6, 32, *33*, 34, 51, **5**:14, 50
Mississippi Company **8**:14, 50
Mississippi River **7**:38
Mithradates I **2**:18, 19, 50
Mittani **1**:19, 50
Mixtecs **4**:15, 51, **5**:22
Moche Culture **2**:27, 30, *34*, 42, 50, **3**:16, 51
Modharites **3**:24
Mogollon Culture **4**:22, *32*, 34, 51, **5**:6, 50
Mohacs, Battle of **6**:15
Molasses Act **8**:19
Moldavia **9**:24, 26
Molly Maguires **9**:38, 51
Mombasa **5**:38, **6**:42, **7**:50, **8**:15
Mombasa, Sultan of **7**:11
Mon **4**:25, **6**:22, 50
Mona Lisa **6**:6, *20*
Monet, Claude **9**:*38*
Mongke **4**:41
Mongolia **3**:40, **10**:9
Mongolian People's Republic **10**:15
Mongols **4**:38, **40–41**, 42, 51, **5**:7, 11, 14, 50, **6**:50, **7**:22, 42, **8**:6, 11, 27
  and China **4**:25, 39, 42, 43, **5**:6, **12–13**
  and India **4**:36, 37
  and Japan **5**:7, 10, 13
  Mamelukes and **5**:7, 8, 9
  see also Genghis Khan; Golden Horde; Timur the Lame
Mon Kingdom **8**:22
Monks Mound **4**:14, 51
Monongahela, Battle of **8**:*28*, 29
Monroe Doctrine **9**:14, *15*, 29, 51
Mons Meg **6**:44
Montano, Francisco **6**:15
Monte Albán **2**:*18*, 50, **3**:24
Montecorvino, John of **5**:14
Montevideo **8**:14
Montezuma I **5**:35
Montezuma II **5**:37, **6**:7, 16
Montfort, Simon de **4**:29, **5**:7
Montgisard, Battle of **4**:34
Montgolfier brothers **8**:*39*
Montreal **7**:22
moon, man on the **10**:34, *36*
Moravia **3**:32, 40
More, Thomas **6**:10, 20
Morgan, Henry **7**:34
Moriscos **6**:50, **7**:7, 10, 50
Mormons **9**:14, 51
Morocco **6**:26, 27, 38, **7**:31, **8**:42, **9**:27, 28, 35, **10**:7, 8, 9
Morse, Samuel **9**:21, 36
Moscow **6**:34, **9**:9
Mossi kingdoms **4**:14, 51, **9**:9, 51
motors, electric **9**:36
Moundsville **4**:38, *39*
movies **10**:*16*, *18*, *19*
Mozambique **4**:23, **6**:7, **8**:19, **10**:27, 38
Mozart, Wolfgang Amadeus **8**:42, *43*
Mu **1**:27, 44
Muawiya **3**:22
Mubarak Shah **5**:34
Mugabe, Robert **10**:39, 41

Mughal Empire 5:28, 51, 6:*6*, 7, 10, 14, 18, 26, 27, 30, 31, 34, 36–37, 39, 42, 50, 7:6, 11, 14, 23, 26, 30, 31, 39, 42, 50, 8:6, 7, 10, *11*, 15, 19, 31, 50, 9:51
Muhammad, and Islam 3:12, 16, 18–19, 23, 6:50
Muhammad Ali 9:7, 8, 13, 14, 18, 19, 21, 10:8
Muhammad al-Muntazar (Twelfth Imam) 3:36
Muhammad ibn Saud 8:31
Muhammad Shah 8:*11*, 19
Mühlberg, Battle of 6:23
Mukden 7:14, 18
mummification 1:11, *24*
Muqaddimah 5:23
Murad I 5:22, 26, 32
Murad II 5:33, 34, 38
Murad III 6:34, 35, 38, 8:6
Murad IV 7:14, *18*, 19
Murad V 9:38
Murasaki, Lady 4:7
Musa 5:*15*, 16, 17, 19
Musa II 5:17
Muslim Brotherhood 10:16
Muslim League 10:22, 51
Mussolini, Benito 10:14, 15
Mustafa I 7:11
Mustafa II 7:43, 8:6
Mustafa III 8:30, 34
Mustafa IV 9:7
Mutamid, al- 3:36
Mutasim, Al- 3:33
Muttawahil, al- 3:36
Muzaffar ud-Din 10:7
Mwenemutapa 4:38, 5:35, 51, 6:13, 51, 7:6, 50
Myanmar (Burma) 4:24, 6:19, 22, *26*, 7:6, 10, 23, 8:7, 26, 30, 9:14, 28, 10:22, 27, 28
Mycenaeans 1:19, 22, 32, 33, 50
Mysore Wars 8:31, 42, 43, 46
Mystic 7:12
Mzilikazi 9:21

NAACP 10:*8*
Nabateans 2:6, 50
Nabopolassar 1:38, 50
Nadir Kuli (Nadir Shah) 8:18, *19*, 23, 50
NAFTA 10:41, 51
Nagabhak I 3:25
Nagasaki 6:8, 34, 39, 7:19, 20, 22, 10:23
Najaf 3:*22*, 7:9
Nakaya Dynasty 6:18, 51
Namibia (Southwest Africa) 10:6, 27
Nam Viet 2:15, 19, 5:30, 34
Nanak 5:38, 6:11, 19
Nanchao, Kingdom of 4:25, 51 5:6, 12, 51
Nanking 6:30
Nan Madol 9:13
Nantes, Edict of 6:42, 7:32, 39, 47
Napier, Charles 9:21
Napoleon III of France 9:26, 27, 28, 29, 34
Napoleon Bonaparte 8:42, 43, 45, 9:6, 7, 8, 9, 10–11
Narashima Saluva 5:42
Narmer 1:*16*
NASA 10:29, 51
Nasir, al- 4:34
Nasir Faraj, al- 5:28
Nasir Muhammad, al- 5:8, *9*
Nasiruddin Muhammad 5:30
Nasr al-Din 9:24, 27, 41, 46
Nasser, Gamel Abdel 10:28
Natal 9:21, 28, 51
Natchez Indians 8:15, 50
Nathan the Wise 8:17
Nations, Battle of the 8:25
Native Land Act 10:9

NATO 10:25, 28, 30, *31*, 33, 51
Nazca culture 2:*10*, 27, 0
Nazis 10:17, 21, 22, 51
Neanderthals 1:6, *7*, 50
Nebuchadrezzar II 1:29, 39, 42, 50
Necho II 1:39, 50
Nectanebo I 2:10
Nehavend 3:17
Nehru, Jawaharlal 10:24, 32, 33
Nelson, Horatio 9:7
Nennius 3:32
Neolithic settlements, Skara Brae 1:*8*, 11
Nepal 5:19, 26, 9:12
Nepos, Julius 2:42
Nero 2:26, 27, 29, 40, 50
Nestorians 3:8, 51
Netherlands 5:42
Neva River, Battle of the 4:43
New Delhi 10:8
New England Confederation 7:23, 50
New France 7:12, 50
New Granada 8:11, 19, 20
New Guinea 1:19, 22, 6:15, 9:15, 41
New Mexico 9:24
New Plymouth 7:12
newspapers, English 8:6, 39
New Sweden 7:26, 51
Newton, Isaac 7:45, 8:16
New York (New Amsterdam) 7:10, 12, *13*, 15, 30, 34, 8:13, 22
New Zealand 3:32, 7:22, 36, 8:31, 42, 9:9, 12, 25, 31, 39, 44, 45
Ngolo Darra 8:30
Nguyen Anh 9:6
Niagara Falls 7:34
Nicaea 4:19, 38, 5:18, 51
Nicaea, Council of 2:50, 3:28, 4:51
Nicaragua 10:9
Nicholas II of Russia 10:7
Nicomedia (Izmit) 5:19
Niepce, Joseph-Nicéphore 9:15
Niger, Pescennius 2:30
Nigeria 5:14, 10:7, 33
Nightingale, Florence 9:*27*
Nihon Shoki 3:26
Nijmegen, Treaty of 7:35
Nile, River 1:51, 9:42
Nile, Battle of the 8:43
Nimrud 1:30
Nineveh 3:16
Nixon, Richard M. 10:30, *35*
Nizam al-Mulk 4:16, 18
Nizip, Battle of 9:20
Nkrumah, Kwame 10:33
Noh theater 5:23, *27*, 51
Nok culture 2:*6*, 7, 18, 50
Noriega, Manuel 10:44
Normans 3:51, 4:6, 12–13, 18, 19, 30, 44
North America
  cultures 4:32–33
  exploration 6:19, 22, 7:6, 7, 10, 27, 31, 34, 8:43, 9:7
  settling of 6:38, *39*, 7:12–13
  Vikings 3:*39*
Northern Wars 7:27
northwest passage 6:38, 51, 7:18, 51, 8:50
Notre Dame Cathedral 4:31
Novgorod 3:36, 46, *47*, 4:43, 52
Nubia 2:26, 38, 3:9, 20, 44, 50
Nubia and Nubians 1:27, 35, 38, 51, 2:7, 3:51
numerals 3:28, 41, 44
Nur al-Din 4:27
Nuremberg trials 10:*25*
Nureyev, Rudolf 10:32
Nurhachi 7:10, 14
Nur Jahan 7:11
nylon 10:20
Nzinga 7:14

Oaxaca 1:23
Obas Akenzua I 8:11
Oceania, settlement 3:42–43
Oda Nobunaga 6:31, 34, 35, 38
Odoacer 2:42, 43, 45
Ogodei 4:41, 42, 43
Ohio Valley 8:22
Ojeda, Olonso de 5:43, 6:9
Oklahoma 9:44
Oklahoma City bombing 10:46
Olaf, *King* 3:45
Old Believers 7:30, *31*
Oleg 3:36, 40, 46–47
Olivares, Count-Duke of 7:*22*, 51
Olmecs 1:22, 30, 31, 34, 36–37, 39, 43, 51, 2:7, 3:52
Olympic Games 1:32, 34, 51, 9:45, 10:30, 35
Omai 8:35
Omar Khayyam 4:10, 15, 17, 23
Omdurman, Battle of 9:47
Onin War 5:38, 42, 51
Opium Wars 9:*20*, 21, 51
Oregon Territory 9:24, 51
Orellana, Francisco de 6:22
Oresme, Nicole 5:23
Organization of American States 10:25
Orhan 5:18, 19
Oriental Entente 10:21
Orsted, Hans Christian 9:12
Orthodox Church
  Eastern 3:52, 4:14, *15*, 52, 6:51, 7:51
  Russian 7:30, 31, 8:8, 52
Osman I (Uthman) 5:10, 18, 33
Osman II 7:11, 14
Osman III 8:*26*
Ostrogoths 2:39, 43, 45, 50, 3:12, 52
Otaker I 4:35
Otto I 3:*44*
Ottomans 5:10, 15, 32–33, 35, 51, 6:7, 27, 51, 7:6, 10, 30, 38, 51, 8:10, 11, 18, 31, 51, 9:12, 15, 18, 19, 34, 39, 46, 51, 10:8, 9, 12, 13, 51
  battles 5:14, 27, 6:10, 15, 34, *35*, 7:43, 8:10, 34, 9:14, 20
  conquests 5:18, 32–33, 39, 42, 6:14, 19, 22, 23, 26, 31, 34, 35, 7:22, 34, 8:14, 15, 9:9, 13, 35
  and the Safavids 6:18, 42, 7:9, 8:22
  see also Janissaries; and names of Ottoman sultans
Oudh 8:15, 51, 9:26, 51
Outremer 4:20, 21, 52
Oyo, Kingdom of 7:18, 51, 8:23, 51

Pacal, *King* 3:17, *34*
Pachacutec 5:37, 6:16
Pacific, War of the 9:41
Pagan 3:33, 4:11, *24*, 25, *25*, 52
pagodas 3:8, *9*, *26*
Pahlavi Dynasty 10:15, 51
paintings, cave/rock 1:*6*, *8*, 31
Pakistan 10:24, 25, 27, 28, 47
Pakubuwono I 8:6, 11
Pala Dynasty 3:37, 52, 4:30, 52
Palenque 3:*33*, 35
Palestine 2:33, 4:18, 19, 22, 9:40, 47, 10:6, 13, 14, 16, 25
Palestine Liberation Organization (PLO) 10:32, 34, 51
Pallava Dynasty 3:13, *24*, 37, 52
Pan-African Conferences 10:13, 51
Panama 4:10, 7:34, 10:44
Panama Canal 9:39, 44, 51, 10:6, 12, 51
Pandya Dynasty 5:7, 10, 51
Panipat, Battles of 6:14, 36, 37
Pankhurst, Emmeline 10:6
Papal States 9:35, 51
paper 2:19, 30, 4:10

papyrus 1:10, *11*, 51
Paracas Culture 1:42
Paraguay 9:8, 9, 17, 10:20, 44
Parakramabahu I 4:*30*, 31
Parakramabahu II 4:43
Parakramabahu III 5:14
Paramardi 4:31
Paris Peace Conference 10:13
Paris, Treaty of
  in 1258 5:6
  in 1763 8:30, 31
  in 1783 8:36, 37, 38
  in 1898 9:47
Paris University 4:27
Park, Mungo 8:42, 51, 9:42
Parks, Rosa 10:28
Parnell, Charles Stewart 9:43
Parsis 3:24
Parthenon 2:7, *8*, 9, 7:39, 51
Parthia and Parthians 2:14, 22, 30, 34, 44, 50
Pascal, Blaise 7:*34*
Passarowitz, Peace of 8:11
Pasteur, Louis 9:*30*
Patagonia 9:40
Patrick, St. 2:41
Paul I of Russia 9:6
Paul of Tarsus 2:27, 40, 41
Pavia, Battle of 6:15
Pazzi family 5:42
Pearl Harbor 9:41, 10:*22*
Peasants' Revolt (England) 5:21, 26, 51
Peasants' War (Germany) 6:*14*, 15
Pedro I of Brazil 9:18
Pedro II of Brazil 9:44
Pegu 6:51, 7:6, 51, 9:28, 51
Peisistratus 1:42
Peloponnesian League 1:42
Peloponnesian Wars 2:9, 51
Pelusium, Battle of 1:42
penicillin 10:15
Peninsular War 9:8, 51
Penn, William 7:13, 38, *39*
Pennsylvania 7:38
Pepi II 1:15, 16
Pepin of Héristal 3:11
Pepin the Short 3:28
Perdiccas 1:51, 2:13, 51
Pericles 2:7, *8*, 51
Perón, Juan 10:28, 35
Perpetua 2:34
Perry, Matthew 9:*26*
Persepolis 2:*7*, 11, 12, 51
Persia 1:25, 51, 2:10, 51, 3:23, 8:14, 9:9, 12, 35
  and Greece 2:6, 8–9, 10
  see also Iran
Peru 1:14, 15, 18, 26, 9:16, 17, 19
Peter III of Aragon 5:10
Peter III of Russia 8:29, 30
Peter the Great 7:42, 8:7, 8–9, 10, 15
Peterloo Massacre 9:12
Peter Nolasco, St. 4:39
Petra 2:6
Petrarch, Francesco 5:19
pharaohs 1:17, *24*, 51
Pharos of Alexandria 2:*13*, 14
Philadelphia 8:42
Philip II of France 4:39
Philip IV (the Fair) of France 5:10, 14
Philip VI of France 5:18
Philip II of Macedon 2:11, 12, 13, 51
Philip III of Macedon 2:13
Philip II of Spain 6:*26*, 27, 30, 31, 38, 39, *40*, 41, 43
Philip III of Spain 7:7
Philip IV of Spain 7:16, 27, 30
Philip V of Spain 8:10
Philip Augustus 4:20, 29, 34
Philip the Good 6:44

Philippines **6**:30, 34, **7**:30, 31, **8**:11, 30, **10**:6, 7, 8, 23, 24, 27
Phoenicians **1**:10, 23, *26*, *30*, 31, 34, 38, 42, 51, **2**:51
phonographs **9**:37, 39
photography **9**:*20*
Phrygians **1**:26, 51
Picasso, Pablo **10**:21
Pilgrims **7**:12, 13, *14*, 51
Pilgrim's Progress **7**:35
pill, birth-control **10**:28
Pinatubo, Mt. **10**:45
Pinochet, Augusto **10**:35, 44
Pires, Thomé **6**:15
Pitt, William, the Elder **8**:29
Piye **1**:25, 34
Pizarro, Francisco **5**:37, **6**:9, 16, *17*, 18, 19, 22
plague **5**:19, **7**:11, 18, 30
  see also Black Death
Plassey, Battle of **8**:27, 29, 32
Plataea, Battle of **2**:9, 51
platinum **8**:23
Plato **2**:8, 10, 51, **6**:51
Plessy v. Ferguson **9**:47
Plotinus **2**:34, 51
Plutarch **2**:30, 51
Plymouth Company **7**:6, 51
Pocahontas **7**:11, 13
Poland **6**:31, **7**:27, **8**:43, **9**:15, 18, 24, 30, **10**:34
  First Partition **8**:25, 34
polio vaccines **10**:28
Polo, Marco **5**:11, *13*
Pol Pot **10**:*38*, 39
Poltava, Battle of **8**:7, 8
Polynesia **4**:*14*, 38, **8**:42
Polynesians **1**:26, 39, 51, **3**:52, **4**:52
  settling Oceania **3**:*42–43*, **4**:35
Pompeii **2**:27, 51, **8**:*23*, 51
Pompey the Great **2**:22, 25, 51
Ponce de Léon, Juan **6**:11
Pondicherry **7**:34, *43*, **8**:28, 32
Pontiac **8**:30, 51
Popol Vuh **6**:*34*, 51
porcelain **3**:25, **4**:42, **5**:19, *24*, *38*, **7**:11, **8**:*26*
Portugal **3**:22, **10**:8, 18
  exploration and trade **6**:6, 7, *8*, *10*, 11, *12*, 14, 27
postal services **8**:14
potatoes **1**:10, **7**:14
  sweet **4**:*14*
Potosí, Mt. **6**:*17*, 23
pottery **1**:10, 14, 15, *22*, 23, 39
Poverty Point Culture **1**:*19*, 51
Powers, Gary **10**:30
Powhatan Confederacy **7**:12, 15, 51
Prague, Compacts of **5**:35
Prague, Defenestration of **7**:11, 16, 47
Prague, Peace of **7**:17
Prague Spring **10**:34, 51
Prajai **6**:23
Presbyterians **7**:19, 51
Prester John **5**:15
printing **3**:25, *40*, **4**:8, 10, 43, **5**:40, **40–41**, **7**:19
Prohibition **10**:13, 20, 52
Prose Edda **4**:39
Protestantism **6**:*24*, *25*, 51, **7**:51
Prussia, rise of **8**:**24–25**
Ptolemy, Claudius **2**:30, **3**:32, 51, **5**:51
Ptolemy I Soter **2**:10, 11, 13, 51
Ptolemy II Philadelphus **2**:14
Pueblo Culture **3**:40, 52, **4**:52, **5**:19, 51
Puerto Rico **6**:7
Pugachev, Yemelyan **8**:34
Pulakesin II **3**:16, 17
pulsars **10**:33
Punic Wars **2**:15, 18, 24, 25, 51
Pure Land Sect **4**:22, 52

Puritans **6**:25, 51, **7**:52
Puyi **10**:8, 9, 20
pyramids **1**:11, 14, 16, *17*
Pyramid of the Sun **3**:*15*
Pyrenees, Treaty of the **7**:27, 32
Pyrrhos **2**:14, 15, 51
Pytheas **2**:11

Qadisiya, Battle of **3**:16, 19
Qaeda, al- **10**:47
Qa'itbay **5**:39
Qajar Dynasty **8**:43, 51, **10**:15
Qalat Bani Hammad **4**:6
Qalawun **5**:8, 9, 10
Qi **1**:38, **3**:8, 52
Qianlong **8**:*19*, 43
Qin and the first emperor **2**:10, 11, **16–17**
Qin Zong **4**:23
Quakers **7**:13, 23, 52, **8**:14, 52
Quebec **7**:6, 7, 12, 42, **8**:*28*, 42, **10**:33
Queen Anne's War **8**:7, 10, 52
Quiché **5**:30, 52, **6**:51
Quiriguá **3**:35
Qutbuttin Aibak **4**:37, 38
Qutuz **5**:7, 8, 9
Quwwat al-Islam mosque **4**:*36*
Qu Yuan **2**:15, 51

Rabin, Yitzhak **10**:44, 46
radio **10**:18
Rahman, Mujibur **10**:38
Rahman ibn Faisal **9**:44
railroads **9**:14, 20, 22, 27, 35, 36, *37*, 41, 46, 47
Rainbow Warrior **10**:41
Rainulf **4**:12
Rajaraja **3**:44, 45
Rajaram **7**:42
Rajasthan **6**:23, 51
Rajendra I **4**:6, 7, 10
Rajputs **6**:31, 37, 51, **7**:52
Ralambo **7**:10
Raleigh, Walter **6**:38, 41, 42, **7**:12
Rama I **8**:38
Rama IV **9**:24
Ramanuja **4**:14
Ramayana **2**:*14*, 51, **4**:52
Ramkhamhaeng **5**:10
Ramses I **1**:24
Ramses II **1**:22, 24, 51
Ramses III **1**:23, 24, 51
Ranjit Singh **8**:43, **9**:*6*, 8, 12, 18, 20
Raphael **6**:20
Rashid, Mulay **7**:*30*, 31
Rashtrakuta Dynasty **3**:29, 52
Ras Tafari **10**:12
Ravenna **2**:42
Ravenna, Battle of **6**:10
Razi, ar- (Rhazes) **3**:40
Raziya **4**:42
Reagan, Ronald **10**:30, *31*, 39, *40*
Red Army Faction **10**:34
Red Cross **9**:30, 51
Red River Rebellion **9**:35
Red River Valley **1**:18, 22
Red Turbans **5**:24, 25, 52
Reform Act **9**:18
Reformation **6**:**24–25**, **51**
refrigerators **9**:36, 37
Rehoboam **1**:27, 28, 51
reindeer **2**:7
Reis, Piri **6**:26
Rembrandt **7**:36, *37*
Renaissance **5**:11, 18, 30, 52, **6**:**20–21**, **51**
Restitution, Edict of **7**:16, 47
Reuter, Paul von **9**:35
revolvers **9**:19
Reza Pahlavi **10**:28, 38
Rhodes **5**:42, **6**:28

Rhodes, Cecil **9**:43, *43*, 44, 46
Rhodesia **9**:43, 46
  Southern **10**:15, 17, 27
Ribault **6**:30
Ricci, Matteo **6**:39, 42
rice **1**:8, 18, 22, 26, 34, 44, **4**:7
Richard I "the Lionheart" **4**:20, *31*, 35
Richard II **5**:26, 27
Richelieu, Cardinal **7**:10, 14, 16, 18
Richmond, Virginia **8**:19
Rif Republic **10**:14
Ripon, Lord **9**:40, 41
Roanoke Island **6**:*38*, *39*, 42, **7**:11
Robert de Hauteville **4**:13
Robespierre **8**:*44*, 45
Robinson Crusoe **8**:11
Roca, Julio **9**:39
Rocket **9**:36
Roger II **4**:27
Roger de Hauteville **4**:19
Rohilkhand, Kingdom of **8**:14, 52
Rolf **4**:12, 29
Rolfe, John **7**:11, 13
Rollo **3**:39
Roman Empire **1**:51, **2**:19, 23, 25, 26, **28–29**, 30, 31
Roman Empire (continued)
  divided **2**:35, 39, *44*
  fall **2**:**44–45**
Romania **9**:40, **10**:44
Romanov Dynasty **7**:10, 52
Romanus **4**:17
Rome **1**:31, 39, **2**:10, 11, 25, 29, **3**:33
  rise of **1**:34, 43, **2**:**24–25**
  sack of (1527) **6**:15
Romulus **2**:*24*, 25, 51
Romulus Augustulus **2**:42
Roosevelt, Franklin D. **10**:22
Roosevelt, Theodore **10**:6, 9
Rose of Lima **7**:34
Roses, Wars of the **5**:*38*, 39, 53
Rosetta Stone **2**:18, **9**:13
Rousseau, Jean-Jacques **8**:*31*
Rowlatt Acts **10**:13
Rozvi Dynasty **6**:51, **7**:26
rubber **7**:11, **9**:22, 37
Rudolf II Of Hungary **6**:35
Rudolf of Hapsburg **5**:7
Rum, Sultanate of **4**:30, 42, 52
Rurik **3**:46
Rus **3**:36, 46, 52
Rushdie, Salman **10**:44
Russia **10**:*13*, 14
  birth of **3**:**46–47**
  drive to the east **7**:19, 23, **40–41**
  Kievan **4**:7, 11, 14
  Time of Troubles **7**:6–7, 10
Russo–Japanese War **10**:6, 7, 52
Russo–Persian Wars **9**:15, 52
Russo–Turkish Wars **8**:31, 35, 38, 52
Ruy Mata **5**:22
Rwanda **10**:45, 46
Ryswick, Treaty of **7**:42

Saadi Dynasty **6**:26, 27, 51, **7**:52
Saavedra, Alvaro de **6**:*9*
Sable Island **6**:43
Sadat, Anwar el- **10**:39
Sadi **5**:7
Safavids **5**:43, **6**:6, 15, 18, 22, 39, 42, 43, 52, **7**:*8*, 14, 52, **8**:15, 52
Saffarid Dynasty **3**:37
Safi I **7**:15, 19, 23
Sahagún, Bernadino de **6**:15, 35
Sahara Desert **1**:16
Said ibn Sultan **9**:8, 18, 27
Saigon **9**:29
Saikuku **7**:39
St. Augustine, Florida **6**:30, **7**:12

St. Bartholomew's Day Massacre **6**:25, 30, 34, 52
St. Basil's Cathedral **6**:32, 33
St. Lawrence River **6**:18, *19*
St. Peter's, Rome **2**:*41*, **6**:6
St. Petersburg **8**:8, 9, **10**:7
Saints, Battle of the **8**:38
Sakas **2**:31, 36, 51
Saladin **4**:20, 30, *31*, 34, 35, 52, **5**:9
Salado Culture **4**:30, 35, 52, **5**:52
Salamis, Battle of **2**:6, 9, *9*, 51
Salazar, António **10**:18
Salem **7**:42
Salerno **3**:40
Salih Ayyub, al- **5**:8
Salonika **5**:33
Samaria **1**:28, 34
Samarqand **5**:*28*, *29*, **9**:34
Samarra **3**:33
Saminids **3**:40
Samnites **1**:40, **2**:11, 14, 52
Samoa **1**:26, **8**:31
Samudragupta **2**:38, 52
samurai **4**:18, 52, **9**:52
Sanchi **2**:*37*
Sancho of Navarre **4**:10
San Diego **8**:31
San Francisco **8**:*20*, **10**:6, 20
Sanjar **4**:31
San Juan Pueblo **6**:43
Sankaracharya **3**:29
Sankoré, Mosque of **5**:*43*
San Martin, José de **9**:16, 17
Sanskrit **1**:52, **2**:14, 15, 31, 39, 52
Santorini **1**:22
Sao Paulo **6**:27
Sao Tome **5**:39
Sappho **1**:39, 52
Saragossa, Treaty of **6**:15, 53
Saratoga, Battle of **8**:35
Sarawak **9**:21
Sardinia **4**:14, **8**:11
Sargon II **1**:34, 35, 52
Sargon the Great **1**:13, 14, 52
Sassanians **2**:34, *35*, 42, 44, 52, **3**:8, 9, 12, 13, 16, *17*, 52
Satakani (Andhra) Dynasty **2**:35
satellites **10**:36
Satsuma Rebellion **9**:39
Saudi Arabia **9**:34, 38, **10**:17, 21
Sa'ud ibn Faisal **9**:34
Saul **1**:28, 52
Savery, Thomas **7**:43
Savonarola, Girolamo **5**:*42*
Saxons **3**:30, 52
Scandinavia, bronze lurs **1**:38
Scheele, Wilhelm **8**:34
Schleswig-Holstein **9**:30
Schmalkaldic League **6**:18, 23, 52
Schouten, Willem **7**:11
scientific revolution **7**:**44–45**
Scipio Africanus **2**:15, 52
Scramble for Africa **9**:28, **42–43**
Scythians **1**:*39*, 52, **2**:52
Sea Peoples **1**:22, 23, 33, 52
Seibal **3**:24
Seleucid Kingdom **2**:11, 13, 14, 18, 32, 52
Seleucus **2**:11, 13, 36, 52
Selim I (the Grim) **6**:10, 11, 28
Selim II (the Sot) **6**:28, 30, 31
Selim III **8**:39, **9**:7, 8
Seljuk Turks **3**:52, **4**:10, 14, 15, **16–17**, 19, 30, 31, 42, 52
Sena Dynasty **4**:22, 30, 53
Senegal **7**:35, 42, **8**:27, 35, 38, **9**:28
Sennacherib **1**:35, 38, 52
Senusret II **1**:18, 24, 52
Senusret III **1**:18
September 11 attacks **10**:47

Serbia 4:34, 5:52, 9:6, 12
Serpent Mound 1:38
Settlement, Act of 8:6
Sevastopol 8:38
Seven Weeks' War 9:31
Seven Wonders of the Ancient World 2:10, 13, 14
Seven Years' War 8:20, 23, 25, 26, 28–29, 30
Severus, Septimus 2:31, 52
Seville, Treaty of 8:15
Sforza famliy 6:20
Shabako 1:35, 52
Shabbetai Tzevi 7:30, 31
Shah Alam II 8:32
Shah Jahan 6:37, 7:14, 15, 18, 19, 26, 30
Shahnama 3:41, 4:7, 53
Shah Rokh 5:30
Shaka 9:12, 13, 14
Shakespeare, William 6:40, 41, 7:10
Shalmaneser III 1:31, 52
Shang Dynasty 1:19, 22, 23, 44, 45, 52
Shang Yang 2:10, 16, 52
Shapur II 2:38, 39, 52
Sharpeville massacre 10:28
Shaykh, al- 6:26, 27
Shen Gua 4:19
Shenyang, palace 7:25
Sherley, Robert 7:9
Sherman, William T. 9:33
Sher Shah Sur 6:19, 22, 23, 52
Shihuangdi 2:15, 16, 17, 52
Shirakawa 4:19
Shir Ali Khan 9:34, 39
Shivaji 7:34, 38
Shizu 8:14, 15, 18
shoguns 4:35, 53, 5:52, 6:52, 7:52, 8:52, 9:31, 52
Shoshenq I 1:25, 26, 28, 52
Shotoku, Prince 3:13, 26, 27
Shunga Dynasty 2:18, 52
shuttles 8:18, 9:22
Siam see Thailand
Siberia 7:19, 23, 40, 41
Sicán art style 3:36, 52
Sicilian Vespers 5:10, 52
Sicily 1:32, 2:7, 9, 3:33, 4:13, 19, 5:10, 8:11
Sicily, Kingdom of 4:42, 44, 45, 5:52
Sierra Leone 7:31, 8:11, 38, 52, 9:8, 20, 46
Sigismund II 6:31
Sigismund III Vasa of Poland and Sweden 6:42
Sikander II Lodi 5:43
Sikhs and Sikhism 5:34, 38, 52, 6:52, 7:34, 43, 52, 8:7, 10, 43, 52, 9:14, 18, 21, 24, 52, 10:52
Sikkim 9:44
Silesia 8:52, 9:21, 52
Silesian Wars 8:22
Silk Road 2:19, 22, 39, 42, 52, 6:6, 52
Silla 3:8, 12, 13, 21, 28, 32, 37, 52
Sima Guang 4:8, 18
Sima Qian 2:22, 52
Simla Deputation 10:7
Sinagua Culture 5:15
Sinan 6:19, 52
Sind 4:35, 9:52
Sind, Ivan 8:30
Singapore 5:19, 9:12, 14, 28
Singhasari Dynasty 5:14
Sino–Japanese War 9:46, 52, 10:52
Sistine Chapel 6:6, 7, 20, 52
Sivaji 7:26, 30
Six Day War 10:33, 52
Skara Brae 1:8, 11, 52
Skopje 5:10
Slave Dynasty 4:36, 37
slavery 7:22, 23, 30, 8:35, 9:27
   end 9:18, 19
   freed slaves 8:38, 9:8, 13, 20, 24, 34

slave trade 6:7, 11, 18, 23, 30, 35, 7:11, 19, 23, 8:12–13, 14, 9:25
   banned 8:42, 9:7, 42
Slavs 3:12, 21, 45, 53
Slovakia 3:40
Slovenia 10:45
smallpox, vaccinations 8:43
Smith, Adam 9:22
Smith, John 7:6, 13
Smithsonian Institution 9:24
Socrates 2:9, 10, 52
Sokolov, Kuzma 8:10
Sokoto Caliphate 9:13, 52, 10:52
Solferino, Battle of 9:27
Solidarity union 10:38, 39, 52
solmization 4:10
Solomon 1:27, 28, 29, 52
Solomonid Dynasty 5:7, 52
Solomonids 5:14
Solomon Islands 2:18
Solon 1:42
Somalia 10:29, 39, 45
Somoza, Anastasio 10:39
Sonam Gyatso 6:34, 35
Song Dynasty 3:44, 53, 4:7, 8–9, 15, 18, 19, 22, 23, 30, 43, 53, 5:12, 52
Songhai 5:17, 26, 38, 42, 52, 6:10, 42, 52, 7:10, 52
Song of Roland 3:28, 4:29
Soninke Dynasty 3:28
Sons of Liberty 8:31
Sophocles 2:8, 52
Soso, Kingdom of 4:34, 38, 42, 53, 5:16, 52
Soto, Hernando de 6:19, 22
South Africa 10:8, 9, 16, 21, 28, 38, 45, 47
Southeast Asian empires 4:24–25
Southern Cult 5:19, 52
Southern Song 4:27
South Pacific Forum 10:35
South Sea Bubble 8:14, 52
Soviet Union (USSR) 10:14, 15, 16, 20, 35
space exploration 10:32, 36–37
space shuttles 10:37, 39, 40, 41
Spain, conquest of 2:28, 3:22, 24, 31
Spanish–American War 9:47, 52
Spanish Civil War 10:21, 52
Spanish Netherlands 6:31, 34, 35, 7:32
Spanish Succession, War of the 7:32, 8:6, 7, 10
Sparta 1:30, 31, 35, 52, 2:6, 8–9
Spartacus 2:25, 52
Speke, John Hanning 9:42
Spenser, Edmund 6:41
Sphinx, the 1:14
Spice Islands (Moluccas) 6:8, 10, 11, 14, 15, 31, 42, 52, 7:14, 30, 31, 50, 8:52
spices and spice trade 6:7, 8, 9, 10, 11, 7:7, 11
spinning wheels 4:10
Spinola, Antonio de 10:35
Sri Lanka (Ceylon) 2:6, 7, 3:33, 45, 5:10, 14, 6:10, 22, 26, 7:26, 8:42, 9:7, 10:25, 27, 28, 35
Srivijaya 3:32, 53, 4:53, 5:52
Stalin, Joseph 10:16, 17, 20, 31
Stamford Bridge, Battle of 4:12, 14
Stamp Act 8:31, 36, 52
stamps, postage 9:20
Stanislaw II of Poland 8:31
Stanley, Henry Morton 9:34, 35
"Star Wars" program 10:30, 37
steamboats and steamships 9:7, 13, 20, 22
steel 8:15, 9:22, 26
Stele of the Vultures 1:14
Stephen Dushan 5:18
Stephenson, George 9:36
Stilicho 2:39, 42
Stone Age 1:52
Stonehenge 1:11, 15, 19, 52
Strabo 2:26, 52
Straits Convention 9:21, 52

Stralsund, Peace of 5:23
Stroesser, Alfredo 10:44
stupas 2:21, 23, 37, 3:53
Stuyvesant, Peter 7:26
Suat 7:7
submarines 7:14
Sucre, Antonio José de 9:16, 17
Sudan 6:6, 10:40, 47
Suez Canal 6:7, 9:26, 34, 38, 10:14, 28
Suez Crisis 10:28, 52
suffrage, women's 9:41, 10:6
Sufi, al- 4:10
Sugar Act 8:30
Suger 4:27
Sui Dynasty 3:13, 53, 4:53
Sukarno, Ahmed 10:16
sukias 5:27
Suleiman II 7:38, 39, 42
Suleiman, Mansa 5:16, 19, 22
Suleimanye Mosque 6:19, 27, 29
Suleiman the Magnificent 5:33, 6:14, 15, 18, 22, 26, 28–29, 30
Sulla, Lucius 2:24
Sultaniya 5:28
Sumatra 3:8, 6:11, 7:39, 9:8
Sumerians 1:10, 12–13, 15, 52
Sunayoshi 7:38, 8:7
Sundiata Keita 4:42, 5:16–17
Sunni Ali 5:38
Sunnis and Shiites 3:22–23
sunspots 2:23
Sun Tzu 2:6
Sun Yat-sen 9:46, 10:8, 14
Suryavarman I 4:25
Suryavarman II 4:23, 24, 25, 30
Susenyos 8:7
Su Shi 4:10
Suttee 3:8
suttee, custom of 3:53, 9:15
Suu Kyi, Aung San 10:45, 46
Svein Forkbeard 3:39
Sviatoslav, Prince 3:44, 46, 47
Swift, Jonathan 8:15
Sydney Harbor Bridge 10:17
Synod of Whitby 3:20
Syria 2:22, 3:19, 4:22, 27, 31, 5:14, 28–29, 35, 8:10, 9:19, 10:14, 15, 24
Syrian Catholic Church 6:43

Tabinshweti 6:19, 23, 26
Tacitus 2:30, 52
Tahmasp I of Persia 6:23, 27, 30, 34
Tahmasp II of Persia 8:19
Taiping Rebellion 9:24, 25, 31, 53
Taiwan (Formosa) 6:11, 7:14, 24, 30, 31, 38, 9:46, 10:24, 41
Taizong 3:17, 4:8
Taizu 3:44, 4:8
Tajikistan 10:16
Taj Mahal 6:37, 7:18, 19, 53
Takakuni Masamoto 6:15
Takrur 3:32, 53, 5:16, 52
Talas River, Battle of the 3:28
Tale of Genji 3:26, 4:7
Taliban 10:46, 47
Talikota, Battle of 6:31
Talmud 2:33, 34, 52
Tamar 4:34
Tambora, Mt. 9:9
Tamil people 3:36, 5:52, 10:53
Tang Dynasty 3:17, 20, 21, 24, 28, 29, 33, 37, 40, 53
Tangier 7:39
Tanguts 4:8, 11
Tannenberg, Battle of 5:30
Tanzania (Tanganyika) 10:12, 13
Tarascan Kingdom 4:22, 53, 5:26, 52
Tarquin I 1:40, 42, 53
Tarquin II 1:39, 43, 53

Tashkent 9:30
Tasman, Abel 7:22, 36, 8:40
Tasmania 7:36, 8:41, 9:7, 27
Tatars (Tartars) 5:52, 6:6, 34, 52, 7:22, 53
Tawfik Pasha 9:40
Tayasal 7:43
Tbilsi (Tiflis) 8:15, 19, 10:44
Teapot Dome scandal 10:15, 53
Teguder Ahmed 5:10
Tehran, embassy hostage crisis 10:39
telegraph 9:31, 36, 37
telephones 9:37, 38
telescopes 6:42, 7:11, 44
television 10:18–19
Telugu language 3:41
Ten Kingdoms 3:40
Tenochtitlán 5:18, 37, 38, 6:14, 16, 17
Ten Years' War 9:34, 53
Teotihuacán 2:27, 30, 35, 38, 42, 53, 3:14–15, 20, 35
Teresa of Avila, St. 6:30
Teresa of Calcutta, Mother 10:47
Terracotta Army 2:15, 16
Tetrarchy 2:44
Teutoburg Forest, Battle of the 2:28
Teutonic Knights 4:20, 21, 38, 42, 43, 52, 5:30, 53, 6:15, 53, 8:53
Texas 8:14, 20, 9:18, 19, 21
Texcoco 5:13
Thailand (Siam) 2:14, 4:6, 6:31, 7:31, 8:35, 52, 9:15, 24, 35, 52, 10:17, 21
Thanksgiving Day 7:11
Thatcher, Margaret 10:39, 40, 41, 45
Thebes 2:10, 11
Theodore II of Ethiopia 9:34
Theodoric 2:43
Theodosius I 2:39
Theophilus 3:33
Thermopylae 2:7, 9, 18, 52
Thirty Years' War 7:11, 14, 15, 16–17, 18, 22
Thomas à Kempis 5:39
Thomas Aquinas 5:7
Thousand Days, War of the 10:6
Three Emperors, League of the 9:35, 50
Three Feudatories 7:34
Three Mile Island 10:38
Thucydides 2:9
Thule culture 4:18, 53
Thutmose I 1:19, 53
Thutmose III 1:22, 53
Tiahuanaco Culture 2:38, 3:8, 16, 53, 4:31
Tiananmen Square 10:44
Tiberius 2:29, 53
Tibet 3:29, 5:6, 7:22, 23, 8:11, 14, 23, 10:6, 9
   Buddhism 3:16, 17, 5:15
   invasions by China 8:26, 10:25
Tiglath-Pileser III 1:28, 34, 53
Tikal 2:19, 35, 42, 53, 3:9, 20, 21, 35
Tilly, Johann 7:16
Timbuktu 5:17, 34, 38, 42
Timurid Dynasty 5:28, 30, 53
Timur the Lame 4:36, 37, 5:22, 27, 28–29, 30
Tinchebray, Battle of 4:22
Tingzhou, Battle of 3:29
Tippu Tib 9:25
Tipu Sultan 8:38, 39, 42, 43, 53
tires, pneumatic 9:37, 43
Titian 6:35
Tizoc 5:42
Tlatelolco 5:11
Tlatilco 1:30
Tlemcen 5:11
Toba 2:53, 4:26
tobacco 7:15
toilets, flush 6:42
Tokugawa Dynasty 7:6, 20, 26, 53, 8:53, 9:34, 53
Tokugawa Ieshige 8:23
Tokugawa Ieyasu 7:6, 10, 21
Tokusei Decree 5:11

Tolstoy, Leo **9**:31
Toltecs **3**:28, *36*, *41*, 44, 53, **4**:7, 31, 53, **5**:14, 53
Tonga **1**:26, **9**:13, **10**:27, 35
Topiltzin **3**:44
Tordesillas, Treaty of **5**:43, *45*, **6**:16, 53
Toshiro **4**:42
Toussaint, François Dominique **8**:*42*, 43
Toussaint L'Ouverture **8**:13
Tower of London **4**:12, 13
Trafalgar, Battle of **9**:7
trains, bullet **10**:10
Trajan **2**:29, 30, 33, 53
transportation revolution **10**:**10**–11
Transvaal **9**:25, 39, 40, 41, 42, 46, 53
Trebizond **4**:38, 53
Trent, Council of **6**:23, 25
Trevithick, Richard **9**:6, 36
Triangle Shirtwaist fire **10**:9
Triple Alliance (1600s) **7**:32–33, 34, 53
Triple Alliance (1800s) **9**:41, 53, **10**:8
Triple Entente **10**:8, 53
Tripoli **5**:8, 9, 11, **6**:26, **8**:53, **9**:6, **10**:9, 40
triremes **2**:*9*
Tristan and Isolde **4**:39
Troy **1**:10, 22, 32, 53
Troyes, Treaty of **5**:31
"True Cross" **3**:16
True Pure Land Sect **4**:39, **5**:43, 53
Truman Doctrine **10**:24, 29, 53
Trundholm **1**:*26*
tsunami **10**:47
Tuareg **5**:17, 34, 53
Tudor Dynasty **5**:42, 53
Tughluq **5**:18
Tughluq Dynasty **5**:*14*, 15, 53
Tughril **4**:35
Tughril-Beg **4**:16, 17
Tughril Khan **5**:7, 10
Tughtigin **4**:22
Tula **3**:*41*, **4**:7, 31
Tulipmania **7**:18, *37*
Tulip Period **8**:11
Tulum **4**:42
Tulunid Dynasty **3**:36, *37*, 53
Tulunids **3**:36
Tuman Bey **6**:10
Tunis **6**:11, 31, 35, **8**:7
Tunisia **9**:40, 42
Tupac Amarú II **8**:*21*, 38
Tupac Yupanqui **5**:37, 39, 42
turbines, water **9**:22
Turkestan **10**:12
Turkey **9**:15, **10**:14, 15, 47
Turner, Nat **9**:18
Tutankhamen **1**:*22*, 24, *25*, 53, **10**:*15*
Twelve Tables, Laws of the **2**:6, 53
Tyler, Wat **5**:26
Tyndale, Matthew **8**:16
Tyndale, William **6**:19, 24, 25
typewriters **9**:15, *38*
Tyre **1**:27, 42, 53, **4**:23, 34
Tyrone, Hugh O'Neill, earl of **6**:42

U2 spy plane incident **10**:30
Ucciali, Treaty of **9**:43
Udayadityavarman II **4**:15
Uganda **9**:46, **10**:35
Ugarit **1**:22, 53
Uighurs **3**:36, 53, **4**:53
Ukbekistan **8**:11
Ukraine **10**:14, 17
Uljaytu, Mahmud **5**:15
Umayyads **3**:17, 20, 22, 23, 25, 53
Uncle Tom's Cabin **9**:25
Union, Act of **8**:7, 46, **9**:6
Union Carbide accident **10**:41
United Arab Republic **10**:29, 53

United Nations **10**:25, 53
United States
  Canadian border **9**:12
  flag **9**:12
  immigrants to **9**:25, 40, **10**:14
Unkiar Skelessi, Treaty of **9**:19
Upanishads **1**:31
Upanishads **1**:53, **2**:6
Uqba ibn Nafi **3**:21
Ur **1**:11, *13*, 27, 53
Urartu **1**:31, 34, 53
Uratu **1**:30
Urban II, *Pope* **1**:20, **4**:19
Ur-Nammu **1**:13, 15
Uruguay **10**:6
Uruk **1**:12, 53
Urukagina of Lagash **1**:15
Urville, Dumont d' **9**:19
Utrecht, Peace (Treaty) of **7**:32, **8**:10, 20
Utrecht, Union of **6**:35, 53
Uzbekistan **9**:34, 35, 38, **10**:12
Uzbeks **6**:53, **7**:15, 18, 53

Valerian **2**:34, 44, 53
Vandals **2**:42, 43, 45, 53, **3**:9, 53
Vanuatu **5**:22
Varangians (Swedish Vikings) **3**:7, 36, 46, *47*, 53
Vargas, Getúlio **10**:15
Vasari, Giorgio **6**:20
Vasudeva **2**:34
Vedas **1**:22, 30, **2**:36, **3**:29, 53
Vedic Age **1**:26
Velazquez, Diego **6**:10, 16
Venezuela **9**:16, 17, **10**:6
Venice **3**:21, **4**:6, **5**:15, 42, **6**:11, 34, **7**:18
Verdun, Treaty of **3**:31, 33, **4**:29
Vermeer, Jan **7**:36
Verrocchio, Andrea del **5**:39
Versailles **7**:*33*, 38, 53, **8**:53
Versailles, First Treaty of (1756) **8**:29
Versailles, Treaty of (1919) **10**:13, 53
Vervins, Treaty of **6**:43
Verwoerd, Hendrik **10**:33
Vesalius, Andreas **6**:23, **7**:44, *45*
Vespucci, Amerigo **5**:43, *45*, **6**:*7*, 8, *9*
Vestini tribe **1**:27
Victor Emmanuel **9**:30
Victoria of Great Britain **9**:19, 38, *42*, **10**:6
Vienna, besieged **6**:15, **7**:38
Vietnam **1**:18, **2**:26, **9**:6, 35, 38, 40, **10**:26, 28, 29, 32
  see also Annam; Champa; Cochin China; Nam Viet
Vietnam War **10**:19, 26, 33, 34, *34*, 35, 38, 53
Viiya **2**:6
Vijaya **5**:23
Vijayanagar **5**:19, 23, 30, 31, 34, *35*, 38, 42, 53, **6**:7, 31, 53
Vijayasena **4**:30
Vikings **3**:32, 33, 36, **38**–**39**, 41, 45, **4**:53, **5**:53
Villa, Pancho **10**:14
Villanova culture **1**:30, 53
Villon, François **5**:39
Vinland **3**:*39*, 45, 53
Virgil **2**:28
Virginia Colony **7**:15, **8**:12
Visigoths **2**:39, 42, 45, 53, **3**:11, 13, 20, 53
Vizcaino, Sebastian **7**:6
Vladimir I **3**:45, *46*, 47, **4**:6
Vlad the Impaler **5**:39, 42
Volstead Act **10**:13
Voltaire **8**:16, *17*, *27*
Von Braun, Werner **10**:36
Voyager (airplane) **10**:40

Wahhabi sect **8**:22, **9**:6, 53
Walachia **9**:24, 26
Waldseemüller, Martin **6**:6, 8

Wales **5**:7, 10
Walesa, Lech **10**:39
Wallace, William **5**:*11*, 15
Wallenstein, Albrecht von **7**:16, *17*, 18
Wall Street Crash **9**:35, **10**:16, 53
Walpole, Robert **8**:*14*, 15
Wang Anshi **4**:8, 15, 18, 22
Wang Mang **2**:26, 53
Wang Wei **3**:21
Wang Yangming **5**:39
Wan-li **6**:34, 38
Warsaw, Battle of **7**:27
Warsaw Pact **10**:28, 30, *31*, 35, 53
washing machines **9**:37
Washington, Booker T. **9**:46
Washington, George **8**:26, 36, *37*, 38, 39
Watergate **10**:35
Waterloo, Battle of **9**:9
Watt, James **9**:22, 23
week, seven-day **4**:6
Wei **2**:35, 39, 42, 53, **3**:53
Wells, Ida B. **9**:45
Wenceslas I **4**:42
West Bank **10**:25, 38, 46
West India Company, Dutch **7**:26, 30, 53
Westminster Abbey **4**:14
Westphalia, Treaty of **7**:*16*, 17, 23, 32, 36
We Zong **4**:23, 26
wheel **1**:12
White Lotus Society **8**:43, 53, **9**:7
White Mountain, Battle of the **7**:14, 16
White Sheep Turkmen **5**:39, 43, **6**:6, 53
Whitney, Eli **8**:*43*
Whittle, Frank **10**:10
Wilberforce, William **9**:18
William I of England **4**:10, 11, 12, 13, 14, 19
William II (William Rufus) of England **4**:13, 22
William II of Germany **9**:44, 47
William III of Orange **7**:34, 36, 37, 42, 53
William of Aquitaine **3**:40
William the Silent **6**:35, 39
Willibrord **3**:25
Wilson, Woodrow **10**:13
Windward Islands **8**:43
witch hunts **5**:42, **7**:*42*
Wolfe, James **8**:27, *28*, 29
Woolens Act **7**:43
World War I **10**:10, *12*, 13, 53
World War II **10**:21–*23*, 53
Worms, Concordat of **4**:23, 44, 45, 47
Worms, Synod of **4**:44
Wounded Knee **9**:*44*
Wright, Orville and Wilber **9**:23, **10**:10, *11*
writing
  cuneiform **1**:*12*, 47, **9**:19, 49
  hieroglyphic **1**:16, 31
Wu Che'eng **6**:42
Wudi **2**:18, 19
Wuh-Teh **3**:44
Wulfram von Eschenbach **4**:38
Wu Sangui **7**:34, *35*
Wu Ti **3**:8
Wu Zetian **3**:21
Wu of Zhou **1**:44
Wycliffe, John **5**:26

Xaltocan **5**:6
Xavier, St. Francis **6**:22, 23, 24, 26, 53, **7**:20
Xenophon **2**:7
Xerxes I **2**:6, 9, 53
Xerxes II **2**:7
Xhosa War, Sixth **9**:19, 53
Xia Dynasty **1**:15, 53
Xuanzang **3**:17

Yakutsk **7**:*41*
Yale University **8**:6
Yamato family **3**:24, 26, 53
Yaqub al Mansur **4**:*34*, 35

Yaqubi, Al- **3**:38
Yaqub Khan **9**:39
Yarmuk, Battle of **3**:16
Yaroslav the Wise **4**:7, *11*, 14
Yasodharman **3**:9
Yayoi Culture **1**:*27*, **2**:53
Yazdigird **2**:42
Yazid I **3**:20
Yeager, Chuck **10**:*24*
Yekumo Amlak **5**:*7*
Yeltsin, Boris **10**:44, 45
Yemen **3**:8
Yemenites **3**:24
Yemrahana Krestos **4**:35
Yermak Timofeyevich **7**:*40*
Yi Dynasty **5**:35
Yongle **5**:25
Yoritomo **4**:35
Yoruba people **4**:14, **9**:*42*
Yoshifusa **3**:36
Yoshimune **8**:10, 14, 22, 23, 26
Yoshitane **6**:15
Young Italy **9**:18, 53
Young Turks **9**:43, 46, 53, **10**:8, 9, 53
Yuan Dynasty **5**:*10*, *12*, 13, 19, 24
Yuan Shikhai **10**:9, 12, *13*, 53
Yugoslavia **10**:15, 47, 53
Yung-lo **5**:30
Yusuf I **5**:18
Yusuf ibn Tashfin **4**:22

Zab, Battle of the **3**:25
Zagwe Dynasty **4**:26, 27, 30, 53, **5**:53
Zand Dynasty **8**:39, 53
Zangi **4**:26, 27
Zanzibar **4**:22, **7**:27, 43, 53, **9**:18, 42, 43
Zapata, Emiliano **10**:13
Zapotecs **1**:*31*, 43, 53, **2**:6, 53, **3**:24, 53, **5**:22, 53
Zara **4**:38
Zara Yakob **5**:35, 38
Zaria **5**:14, 53
Zedekiah **1**:50
Zeng Gongliang **4**:11
Zenj rebellion **3**:36
Zenobia **2**:34, 35, 53
Zenta, Battle of **7**:43
Zeydis **6**:31, 53
Zhagawa people **3**:17
Zheng-he **5**:30, 31
Zhenzong **4**:8, 9
Zhongdu **5**:12
Zhou Dynasty **1**:44–45, 53 **2**:7, 16, 53, **3**:12
Zhou Enlai **10**:16, 35
Zhu Yuanzhang **5**:23, 24–25
ziggurats **1**:10, *11*, 53
Zimbabwe **3**:45, **4**:38, *39*, **10**:39, 41
Zollverein **9**:19, 53
Zoroaster **1**:53
Zoroastrians **1**:42, 53, **2**:42, 43, 53, **3**:24, 53
Zsitvatörök, Treaty of **7**:6
Zulus **6**:13, **9**:*12*, 13, 14, 21, 53
Zulu War **9**:38, *39*, 53
Zwingli, Ulrich **6**:11, 18